Cahir History & Stories

Seanie Lonergan

DEDICATION

For Mag.....who else.

ACKNOWLEDGEMENT

People that helped me fill between the covers of this book over the last few years will be glad that I no longer will be pestering them.

Thanks, in no particular order…Michael Peters and his computer.

Denis landy, John Quirke, Mossie Casey, Rosalynd Hurst, Ger'O Brien for his collection, John Mackey.(for Jaysus sake will you write a book). Paddy Mahon, Jerry Sheehan the fount of all knowledge about Cahir.Kieran Ryan, Michael Keating, Mary O' Donnell…here are two jotters fill them up.

This could not have been done without the generosity of the people that donated on Go Fund Me and privately. I thank you.

Ber in Dublin for getting the ball rolling.

ABOUT THE AUTHOR

Sean Lonergan lives in Cahir all his life. Married to Mag and has 5 children. Was involved in Politics, but has now retired and has taken up light woodwork in his workshop.He is interested in all local history and with a friend of his makes videos for YouTube about local historical sites.

INTRODUCTION

CAHIR

This book began in the year of 2024 when the population of Cahir was around 4.500 souls, In the year 1881 the number of people was 2,469 and the town was owned by a Lady Margaret Charteris. It was this woman that commissioned the fountain in the town square in memory of her husband. The project cost 3.000 pounds at the time, the work was carried out by local people, the trench was dug by pick and shovel from Scaragh wood to the Square in town a distance of 2 miles, Irish miles.

Before that event water was drawn from the river Suir and freshwater wells and springs. In later times more pipe was added and outside water tap stands, were in use for years. At that time all houses had at least one water bucket and if one was lucky an enamel bucket.

SOCIETY OF FRIENDS

Like most towns along the rivers. milling took place and was mostly carried out by the Quakers a very resourceful people, most of the big houses belong to these people, they also were very active during the famine in saving thousands of starving victims, by running soup kitchens and like the poor house at Tincurry, taking care of hundreds of starving children…a story we will learn about later. In 1697 the Quakers had a meeting house [they did not have chapels or churches] in Knockgraffon then in Kilcommon and later in Garryroan before building the Meeting house on the Tipperary road on Abbey St. in 1835. At Kilcommon the Quaker graveyard, Garrainalive it is called, all the headstones are all of equal dimensions. They are all facing the same point of the compass, all that is except one and the reason for that is that the poor unfortunate took his own life. The Quaker family in Garryroan were called Fennell. Joshua was somewhat of a Biologist and because of his work had the vegetable Fennel called after him, they also grew tobacco and the field at Whitechurch is still called : the tobacco field:

Being pacifists they did not defend their land when Oliver Cromwell stopped by. The Lord Protector robbed all their livestock and destroyed all the crops. Cromwell was on his way to Cahir Castle where he was about to give rise to the insult, Shuneen Cahir.

Cahir castle was visited by other tyrants, The Earl of Essex in 1641 gave the fort a pounding… in 1647 Lord Inchiquin arrived with his cannons and blew the side walls near the entrance gate, and of course Oliver Cromwell gave the ultimatum come out and I will spare you.

The tyrant's behaviour was such in Wexford where he killed 2,000 and in Drogheda murdered 3,000 people. In both of these towns he ordered none to be spared. This was in 1640. Cahir Castle was built in 1220 and is still sound. The castle grounds extended up to the AIB bank, at the rear of the bank on their grounds are 3 underground Jail cells and a high walled compound. The compound or yard still has the iron ring shackles used to tether prisoners during the day. It was here that Willie Brennan and the White Pedlar were held before being taken to Clonmel for court and hanging…we will learn more about these two later…

G.K. Chesterton said.

That Cromwells visit to Ireland was that the Irish never forget it.

And that the English never remember it.

THE FEVER HOSPITAL

The fever hospital is on the Cork road at Carrigeen still occupied but not as a hospital. It was a last resort during the Famine where the starving and diseased people..men ..women and children died after a short spell in the facility, the bodies were brought a few yards outside in the field and interred, most of them without coffins. A British officer, a doctor, resigned his commission in the Barracks and went to work without pay in an attempt to save or give professional help to the poor people. Michael Daniels deserves a hero mention for giving his young life for others.

A not so comforting thought is that during the famine, Kennedys Hospital as it was called, is that for every 100 brought in there, 99 died, every inch of the field claims a body, some of which were interred half dead. Most without coffins and the burial party were so emaciated they could barely function.

THE STONE PILLARS

A hidden gem for many years is a pair of standing stones at Ballymacadam and Mooneraha, everyone thought that they were cattle scratching stones, not many at the time knew the reason for these until the 1930 folklore commission stories were published. This pair of pillars are about 300 metres apart on separate hills. Each one is identical in stature except for the inscriptions. One inscription is praise of Daniel O Connell and the other is a monument to Robert Peel, both very much enemies.

Daniel O Connell did however spend one night in Cahir and was not very well received being a garrison town. He stayed in Mullaney's House at the top of the Square on his way to Carrick on Suir. Charles Bianconi was his driver.

There was a wealthy builder called Cusac that built some of the houses in the town; he had 800 acres leased from the estate. In Dillons Bohreen there lived a sculptor who plied his trade in Clonmel and was considered the best around, he was approached by Cusac who offered him 5 pounds to turn out a pillar for him, this he duly did and after the monument was erected he ordered another of Peel.

Peels pillar was erected and caused a stir as there was no reason for It. Cusac was a bit of a prankster and the wealthy indulged in this kind of thing. These were known as follies.

Robert Peel was MP for Cashel even though he was never in Ireland.

Just for the uninformed, Peel was responsible for forming the British Police force……hence, The Peelers…

There is another train of thought that Daniel O'Connell did make a speech along the Convent road as we call it. This road was the main Clonmel road. Some years ago a large machine was in collision with one of the pillars and it has been lying at an angle since.

There was another train of thought: it was that Cusac erected the Peel pillar first and due to the pressure of O Connells followers in Cahir he complied and erected one to the Liberator. I decided to acknowledge both versions.

CAHIR BRITISH ARMY BARRACKS

This was one of the biggest barracks in Tipperary. It was mainly a cavalry post; it housed the South Irish Horse and the 11th and 12th hussars as well as the Light Brigade; it had accommodation for 1000 personnel .

Across the road from the east gate there was a village comprising two saddlers and leather workers, feed and fodder stores, a bakery and two pubs. Mrs Alicia Hennessy was an army baker and ran a family grocer shop..Jeremiah Ryan was a spirit merchant and had a pub and shop. Kellys was the other bar. The barracks was built in 1811 and lasted until the civil war. It was burned by republicans and as soon as the smoke cleared the locals availed of anything they could. For miles around there is hardly a farm that has not got anything made of cast iron.

The light Brigade returned here following the Crimean war and the famous Charge of the Light Brigade. Bringing with them horses called Crimea Bob and Donkey who now are buried under the beef plant.

In 2011, I interviewed a woman called Mir Kennedy, she told me that she stood in the Square and watched the British soldiers from the barracks marching off to the FIRST world war, the noise was deafening from the gun carriages, horses and the Army Bands. There is an old photo of the Square without the trees, the photo was colourized. It has a girl in a white apron and carrying a little basket standing beside the fountain. That girl is Mir Kennedy delivering meat from the butchers.

In 2011 This woman was 101 years old.

THE WIT OF THE LAWMAKER

In 1830 a newly arrived young Cahir man educated in England called Sergeant who recently passed his bar exams was eager to make a name for himself in the Irish courts. He approached a wily old magistrate and posed the following question. Your lordship what is the extreme penalty for bigamy in Ireland.? The wily old head thought for a few seconds and said..Two mothers in law.

ST. MARY'S CATHOLIC CHURCH

Built in 1839 beside the site of another older church, the first Parish Priest was a Fr. Tobin.

While the church was being built, the Priest and other members of the cloth resided in Suirvale House on the Cashel road and because of their presence the road became known as the Priests Road.

CAHIR BOYS NATIONAL SCHOOL

Erasmus Smith in building this school constructed the most expensive structure in Tipperary at a cost of 1.034 pounds in 1818. The school was multi-denominational with 131 children of which 90 were catholic. More rooms were added in the 1830s. The famous architect John Nash, who designed St.Paul's Church of Ireland and the Swiss Cottage was called upon to draw plans for the school.

Another notable building by John Nash is Buckingham Palace in London.

RAILWAY STATION

One of the most imposing buildings in town it was opened on the 1st May 1852 and was a hive of activity in its heyday. Everything came by rail and was delivered around the town by horse and cart, two of the last men that I remember delivering were Gerry Moore and Seanie Halloran.

There were two rail accidents on the Viaduct, one in 1955 when the beet train went down. Cornelius Kelly and Francis Frahill lost their lives. The other was in 2003, this time it was the cement wagons that crashed through. There were no casualties on this occasion. The line was closed for a few years while repairs were carried out.

There was living accommodation in the railway building for the Station Master. Ronnie Bearmore was the last Station Master and lived there with his family. Ronnies father was a British soldier.

Ronnie was born in India, a very popular man with everyone, he used to say that he was the only Indian among the Cowboys .

BENGURRAGH

Home of some of the best soccer players for Cahir Park FC and abroad. A circle of 31 houses built in the 1940s saw an exodus after the closure of the Cahir Mills, whole families moved to other towns, England and further,

Some that I remember were The Cronins to England, the Ryans to New Zealand, the McGraths to Australia, the Dillons to Dublin. There were two families of McGraths called the Bakers and the Wallens.

A poll conducted in 2024 found that there were 6 school children in Bengurrah, compared to 142 scholars in 1963.

Miss O'Keeffe was a music teacher that had a full calendar of students, her neighbours Danny Buckley and Ellen Keys sold fish on the square every friday, Danny had a cure for Thrush and affected people had to go to him at six in the morning before his breakfast.

The green in the centre was busy after school as football was played by all both boys and girls ... .golden days.

SRAID NA GCUIC

Translated as the Road of the Cuckoos, it was a line of 19 houses that were taken down in 1969 to make room for Avondale Court on the Tipperary road. The houses were in bad condition with tin roofs over thatch, mud walls and half doors

Some of the surnames of the occupants were Lonergan, Dee, Duggan, Dempsey, O Brien, Leonard, Butler. Burke, Cagney, Fitzgerald, Walsh. and not forgetting Kitty the Hare, a little woman who was always in a good mood and pinned to her coat were holy medals, she always wore boots and a tam. [beret]

There were two massive Chestnut trees hard by the road and they were known as the poison trees. Originally these houses would have belonged to the Rochford estate. The estate was then owned by a succession of different people.

ENTERTAINMENT

The Capitol cinema was on the Clonmel road and fell to the advent of Television. Most of this information came from a gentleman called Gerry Sheehan a native of the town.

The Capitol cinema closed on the 17th January 1970. The last picture shown was ..The Silencers..starring Dean Martin. The last manager was Tommy Shine and the second last was Brendan Mulcair from Thurles, we cannot forget Bridie Lonergan and Phil Buckley who looked after the tickets.

The Savoy was on Abbey Street and the last picture shown then was ..One For The Post..starring George Formby, the small picture that night was,,,, From The Manger To The Cross,,,, and the Savoy closed in 1946.

At the top of the Square there was a grocery shop and public house called Mulcahys, at the rear of the building was a large hall that was used to show silent films in 1912 and doubled up as a ballroom, mostly used by the British soldiers from the barracks.

After the Capitol cinema closed, Tommy Shine purchased a projector and had mobile picture shows in the towns and villages in the vicinity but the Television won out.

DANCING

Cahir was not short of Ballrooms a century ago, a lot of the big houses had their own.

The poor of course would not be outdone, they danced in each other's houses as well as cross roads that were called stages, every cross road had a dance when the weather was fine.

The great hall in the Cahir castle was used up to the late 60s the Parochial hall in later times.

The mecca of all was the Arcadia on the Clogheen road. Busloads of people of all ages came from the surrounding towns and as far away as Dromkeen, the pubs were buzzing on weekends.

Showbands.. The Royal, The Miami, Brush Shiels, the Champions, The Dixies, Martin Flynn and the Editors, Mick Delahunty, Donie Collins and even Joe Louis the world champion boxer paid a visit.

HIGHWAYMEN

Willie Brennan came from Kilmurray on the banks of the Blackwater, his parents worked for the estate on which they lived. The recruiting Sergeant from Fermoy came around looking for recruits for the Cavalry in the local barracks. Willie was taken in by the uniforms and the false promises of a romantic life. He was very young and was not long turning against army life, our lad could not keep his hands off anything shiny like gold or silver. He stole an officer's gold watch and decided to desert with a price on his head, because the punishment was whipping. Being an accomplished horseman he evaded capture for a long time. As the song says it was on the Kilworth mountains he began his wild career. His area, if one can call it that, extended from beyond Fermoy to Cashel. The mayor of Cashel was unlucky to have a gold chain around his neck because Willie was on the prowl, he tried to steal the chain but was apprehended and was to be hanged. Willie's wife was a strong woman and when she heard what happened she rode to Cashel from Tincurry. On her way she picked up a blunderbuss and was successful in rescuing her husband. Willie met and became partners with another robber called the White Pedlar,..Paddy Hogan..Like all that chose that way of life they have a very short career. On the Galtee mountain over Tincurry, Willie and his wife and three children were building a homestead, a mud cabin that has long since fallen to the ground. There is a stretch of mountain that is called Brennan's ditch in the townland of Quarryhole. More than once Willie displayed a madness or reckless attitude, he formed a plan to rob Jacksons of Millgrove, a house not a half mile from where he planned to live. Jackson was an enterprising Quaker who had a lot of projects going on at that time. He was building a flax mill and a linen mill. Willie looked at this as an opportunity of fast money. He and his fellow robber entered Millgrove in broad daylight, they both gave Jackson a very brutal beating. The maid heard the rumpus and ran for help. She encountered the militia that were already out looking for the pair. The two robbers had the money and were making their way towards Cahir. They rode as far as Clonmore where they hid out.

A woman that was in the pay of the British had the agreed sign on display, to let the Militia know that Brennan was near. The sign was a shirt hanging by the tails. The British method of drying. The militia got ready to do battle and rode into a farmers yard where they discovered the culprits, a shootout ensued and Brennan lost his finger. Both were taken prisoner.

They were taken to the Jail cells at Cahir Castle for the night. In the morning they were taken to Clonmel. Both were sentenced to be hanged the following day.

In the morning the two men were placed on a horse cart with ropes around their necks. Willie, fearless to the last, joked with the crowd, the Pedlar however did not find it amusing. The horse was whipped and ran with the cart. The men swung for a minute and were still.

Willie Brennan was interred at Kilcrumper cemetery outside Fermoy. The Cortege grew in size every mile of the road, mourners walked and rode horseback from Clonmel and farther all the way to near Fermoy, by the time it got to the final resting place it was almost 2 miles long. He captured the small man's imagination and he bucked the trend, songs were sung all around the world brought over by the enlisted men.

This account was gleaned from a man called George Farmer that served in the British army with Brennan and was part of the militia that captured him and was at his execution.

Tis of a brave young highwayman this story I will tell

Brennan on the moor, Brennan on the moor

Bold brave and undaunted

Was young Brennan on the moor.

Twas on the Kilworth Mountains he commenced his wild career

And many a wealthy nobleman

Before him shook with fear.

April 1809 saw the last of Brennan and Hogan; it is not recorded where Hogan was buried.

DID YOU KNOW

Barrack St, where the Fire Station is built, used to be a sports field and a place where the Circus used to pitch its Big Top. Known to all as Loobys field.

You will notice on the wall at the top of Barrack Street that windows and doors were blocked up. There were several working mens houses that did not fit with her Ladyship's idea of neighbours so she had them removed.

During the British occupation there was a Golf Course at Ballydrehid beside the Khyber pass.

There were two swimming places in the Suir, one was called the Sandy Bank and the other was accessible under the viaduct called the Sandy Bottom.

Cahir was a large basket making centre, most of the willows were grown in the Osiery near the Viaduct. The willows were also sold to other towns. A Mr.. Burke and a Mr. Kenneally were adept at weaving potato baskets with handles, full time.

Cahir Park FC. Their magnificent entrance gates were the original way into the Cahir House now the Hotel.

There was a Cricket Club at Cahir Park and it is reported that Bram Stoker played there, as everyone knows Stoker wrote the novel Dracula.

The first house on the Mall used to be a Convent; the nuns waited until 1888 to move to the new convent on Pearse St. The new one took 10 years to build.

A place near Garryclogher called Glen Righ [Kings Glen] where Geoffrey Keating went into hiding, a cave with 3 spaces where he lived for a long time on the run .

According to legend a Mermaid called to Clonmore and told the locals that 3 cows would come around. Every place the cows went, a place would be named after them, one of these places is Loch-na-Bo. The lake of the cows.

There is rock in Scarragh Wood,it is an ancient burial place, legend has it that it was thrown from the Knockmealdown Mountains and landed there, and that it was called Garran Ban.

FOLKLORE

There is a field near our house in Garryroan called the stone field, in the centre of the field there is a huge heap of stones, said to have been collected by the Danes to be burned so that the local people could not build houses. However they were out of luck, Brian Boru was on his way to Knockgraffon and ran them off.

They say that there is gold buried there, but it is guarded by a man about a foot tall. He is always walking the field at night.....Tommy Finn 1930.

REALITY

The mounds of stones are in fact Cairns or ancient graves and are said to be older than the Pyramids. They are located in Garryroan and there are two of them. The larger of the two has three chambers and the smaller has two. Handed down reports say that there was a battle and the Chieftains that were killed are interred there. The custom for thousands of years was to bring a stone and put it on the mound as a mark of respect. Archaeologists would have to tunnel their way in to find out for sure about the dead.

GO SLOWLY

The S bends at Kilcommon are known by the locals as the Go Slowlys.

Because the first road signs following an accident were erected there. The signs were cast iron letters with red glass buttons in the letters that spelt out GO SLOWLY.

TRUST ME

Unfortunately I have to withhold the real names but it will not affect the story, this tale I promise is fact.

In the late 1930s there was a woman that had a one nighter with a newly elected local Councillor for the Cahir area and she fell pregnant. She had a bouncing baby boy and she approached the man for maintenance and as expected he refused. This led to a court appearance where the judgement fell in her favour, she was awarded a half crown a week. This was the 1930s and a nice sum.

To humiliate her she had to go to the pub to collect every week and walk the gauntlet of his friends. This went on for about 6 years, and then she used to send the boy himself.

The years passed and one day the man asked the strapping young boy his age, the lad answered that on the following Wednesday he would be 18. Well then said the man I will no longer be your father after Wednesday. The boy was a little confused and told his mother at home. The mother said son, when you meet him again, tell him that he …... never was.

HALLELUJAH

In the 1990s, another true story that I was asked to withhold the real name. Peg was living a little up the Galtees on her own; her husband was gone to his maker for a long time, times were hard.

One day the Jehovah Witnesses knocked on her door convincing Peg that they were true saviours of her soul. They asked if she needed anything, shur said " Peg I have naught. They went to town and got her lots of groceries and clothes, new aprons and the like. They kept this up for a long time, all summer in fact. Their plan of course was to entice Peg to become one of them.

Peg was never as well off and thanked them. They asked Peg what she thought of them and Peg said that she knew all her prayers to the Virgin Mary would pay off. Told to me by John O Donnell Snr. Clonmore.

PADDY EGAN

Paddy, like numerous Irish, emigrated to England because things were tough in Ireland in the late 1930s. All of Paddy's brothers went there. They were there during the war and worked at lots of mechanical jobs. Paddy and his brother John married sisters and saved to come home.

Before he got married he and his brother George shared an upstairs room, during the war the room had black out curtains to contain the light.

One night there was an air raid, the sirens were screaming the bombers would be soon overhead. The drill was that everyone rushed to the air raid shelter in the park. George and Paddy were at their supper. Paddy grabbed his cap and hit down the stairs, on the pavement he waited for George, no sign of his brother. Paddy ran back up the stairs to see George feeling around the table in the half dark. What the hell are you doing, screamed Paddy?. George said that he was looking for his false teeth.

For God's sake says Paddy its bombs they are dropping not sandwiches.

Only that he did not say. For God's sake….

JOHNNY O' BRIEN

Like almost a hundred thousand of his countrymen Johnny joined the British army during the second world war. He was born and reared on the mountain road. Returning home after the war, his main aim in life was to be the keeper of the First World War monument. Johnny passed away in 2018 at the age of 95,...He told me this story

The emergency brought a lot of outsiders with the 13th battalion and they took up with the local women, A favourite haunt was the mountain on a summer day, Fruit was practically non existent then, The soldier and his beau entered a shop and tried to buy an orange, The shopkeeper said that the oranges were only for pregnant women. What did he say she asked? We will get it on the way back, replied the soldier.

KHYBER PASS

So called because the British army returnees said that it resembled the famous pass between Pakistan and Afghanistan.

Our pass is to be found on the Tipperary road at Ballydrehid, it was dug by very primitive machinery to allow the railway to get through the mountain. The engineering was a marvel for its time, the earth that was dug out was carried to fill the mound before the Viaduct. The track had to be lifted twenty five metres at one end and dug down at the other end This was all done in the early 1850s. The name will not be found on any map but all the locals know it by nothing else.

A CURE IN SLEEP

Another practice that was prevalent in my younger days was people going to bed for years, not because they are injured or sick outwardly. I knew several men and women that stayed in bed for a long time.

In 2023 I met a man that I had not seen for years and asked him where he had been..I took to the bed was his answer and that was what it was called…Taking to the bed…

One of the writer John B Keane stories was of a woman taking to the bed.

DON'T TALK TO ME

This is a true account, gleaned from a book about the famine. During The Great Hunger a lot of people made money and acquired a lot of land rather cheaply. One such man purchased land from a poor family that was emigrating. When things improved after the Hunger there was a little movement with money.

The land that he bought was about 10 miles over the mountain and a nosey neighbour asked him of his plans for it.

Deed I am sorry that I came by it, for it would cost me money. If I had to work that land …..I would have to pay someone to listen to and talk to my wife for she would be on her own.

THE CHILDREN'S FAMINE HOUSE

Brookfield was the proper title for the poorhouse location beside Tincurry. We are back to the Quakers again and their work at Tincurry guarantees them a place in heaven. The site is about 3 miles out the Cork road.

The poorhouse was part of the Poor Law Union and they had a little factory at Brookfield for the girls where they learned sewing and knitting. The boys were learning how to have a garden, with implements to suit their stature and grow their own.

There were 600 children at any one time. The food consisted mainly of watery soup with vegetables if they were available. A large cast iron pot boiled all they had. In the evening all the children lined up with their little bowls for whatever was cooking..

Mortality was very high, there was a report of 21 dying in one week. The burial place was up the hill on the side of the barren mountain; it is estimated that there are up to 1800 little bodies buried there.

There was a fire and the factory being thatched went up like tinder. The children were moved to Clogheen where the Hospital is now.

One child remained because he was too sick to be moved. Among his ailments he had Scrofula,,,he lasted a few days and was the last child to be buried from the poorhouse, in the Tincurry burial ground, he was seven years old……John Griffin.

Some children as soon as they felt better used to run away for a while, two such orphans were returned after running away. Their names were Lonergan and Riordan.

A monument was erected to the memory of these poor mites because there was a fear they would be forgotten, after 150 years, the Monument was erected by Ed Riordan and Seanie Lonergan.

A few hundred yards down the road at Millgrove the Quakers ran a soup kitchen. Ed Riordan has written a fantastic account of the famine... called Famine in the Valley. It is online.

GINCHY TERRACE

Called after a village and first world war battle in France.

The Irish Soldiers And Sailors Land Trust were responsible for supplying these 8 houses in Lisava Cahir on the mountain road.

The houses were to be built on the Clonmel road but the decision was changed to the present location. The tenders were received and the contract was awarded to..Messers Roche..Morrissey and Kennedy of Clonmel for the 8 houses, this was on October 2nd 1926.

When they were completed the rent was 4s-6d per week plus rates.

When the husband died the wife got the house for her lifetime. Then it was given to another ex-service person. But this changed later.

There was a clash with the authorities over the rent, some of which was returned and then there was no rent.

Later a payment of 5 pounds would guarantee a family member could purchase the house. If this did not happen the trust would sell the property

CAHIR PARK HOUSE

On the morning of May 11th 1963 Andy Buckley was on his way to work in the Cahir Bakeries at 6 am, when he saw smoke coming from Cahir Park House, he alerted Paddy Dalton and the panic was on to get the fire brigades. Cahir fire brigade was on the scene in minutes, joined by the Clonmel men a half hour later.

The great house was beyond saving and was totally destroyed.

Paddy Dalton said that he heard explosions as the house went up. The firemen fought the blaze through the day but to no avail.

The great house was due to open as a hotel in another week by the Trust House Forte Group. The finishing touches were under way and the stationery was already printed.

The Nationalist Newspaper reporter said that the enormous sum of 55,000 pounds was lost in preparation of a magnificent modern hotel. There is no doubt that setting and location would never be matched in all of Ireland. There were rumours and whispers of sabotage or malicious intent but this was never proven.

In the estates heyday there was a lot of employment between the big house and the estate with its farm, plenty of employment but not plenty of money, the locals believed in the adage little and often. In 1933 a kitchen maid's wages were £22 a year, while the cook took home £70 a year and this was for a six and a half day week. The staff were allowed to attend Mass if they hurried back over the spring bridge.

Paddy Dalton was Col.Charteris driver and was armed with a revolver, all his family worked for the estate, as did most of the town.

There was a little man that was a jeweller and clockmaker in Wellington Street now Pearse St. His name was Matty Woulfe and his job every week was to wind the clocks in the big house. He had to carry a small step ladder to reach the grandfather clocks. The house gardens were looked after by permanent staff and there were

Peacocks always wandering around. Mr Charteris bred swans down by the Swiss Cottage and there are photos of a few black swans in the group.. Gamekeepers were employed to guard the Fishing areas and the Pheasant breeding cover at Garryroan. On June 7th 1962 an auction in the old farmyard of contents and livestock took place in Kilcommon, the auction needed three Auctioneers to complete the sale, a Mr McCarthy...C.O Dwyer and D.Butler Miavi.

POSTMEN ON BIKES

Tom Burke arrived in Cahir with the 13th battalion from Ballygarrett in Wexford. He was one of the first Postal van drivers when the bicycles were no longer used. He told me that his round took in Ballybrado House. After a few days Mrs Craig-White complained that he had not brought her morning paper ... .Tom said that it was not part of his job as he was the mailman. She asked if Tom took a drink and he replied that he was partial to a dram.......The Lady handed Tom a bottle of Black and White whiskey,,,, she got her paper delivered after that.

Tom married Winnie Flynn daughter of Kevin .. of Showband fame and Tom and Winnie passed away only 2 months apart in Jan 2010 following a long and happy life.

HOLY WELLS

On the Tipperary road out of Cahir is a well Called TOBAR IOSA, translated as Baby Jesus Well. In the not so distant past people flocked to these places, they were considered as Holy areas. In times gone by soldiers that were going off to war always visited, no matter what religious persuasion.In the penal times they were used by the faithful to practise their religion. in hiding from the British tyrants.

Every well it is thought to have a cure, blindness and warts seem to be at the top of the ailments..

The Cahir well was a grand peaceful spot until vandals struck, they destroyed the lovely ambience of the once beautiful setting.

MURDER IN THE BARRACKS

In 1896 saw the hanging in Clonmel of a soldier in the British army in Cahir Barracks. Private Kenny, as he was known, murdered a fellow soldier named Private Goodwin.The killing took place in one of the underground kitchens at Kilcommon. He was arrested and tried and was found guilty, he was sentenced to hang.

During the trial it came to be that Kenny was actually a German named Kreutz, who had deserted the German army and joined the Russian army. He ran from the russians and made his way to

England, where he joined the 3rd Hussars, under the alias of Williams he then deserted and made his way to Dublin where he joined the Fusiliers, under the alias of Kenny the was then moved to the 8th Hussars in Cahir.

He was hanged in Clonmel at 12 o'clock noon; it is believed that he helped the hangman to put on the straps that are used in such occasions.

At the minute of his hanging the Regiment formed two lines facing each other, in the parade ground they had an effigy made of Kenny/Kreutz and it was kicked down the lines of his fellow soldiers. This was tradition as the hanged man had brought disgrace on the 8th Hussars.....Private Kenny was 27 years old.

THE PARADE FIELD

Going south from the Barracks at Clonmore is the Parade Field, so called because of the 80 acre flat space that the Cavalry drilled their sturdy war horses..

There is a painting that depicts the Light Brigade, composed of 600 grey horses and the South Irish Horse, the Hussars both the 8th and 12th going through their paces in the field. The field was used by the British as long as the Barracks was there.

Through the years the field was used as an Airfield and there are photographs of the old bi-winged aeroplanes with their crews. On occasions locals would pay a half crown to fly around for a short while. That was in the 1930s.

On 8th July 2005 two Americans Peter Mc MIllan and John Lanoue,. were emulating the Alcock and Brown crossing of the Atlantic. They completed the journey as planned. On this occasion they were to fly from Shannon to Walcs, whcn they developed a problem with their replica Vimy Aircraft. From their altitude they saw the Parade and did an emergency landing there.

Eamon Williams was on hand to help them arrange mechanical aid to get them airborne again. Eamon and his good lady Nellie gave the pair a place to sleep for the night. The drinks cabinet was opened and the beds saw very little use that night. Irish Hospitality.

CANADIAN MOUNTED POLICE

General Sir William Francis Butler was born in Ballyslateen in 1838. Was Irish and Catholic, is credited with forming the Mounties during his posting in Canada. His wife was the famous war artist that painted the… Charge of the Light Brigade..he had a very distinguished career and was a great admirer of Charles Parnell and promoted home rule. He died at Bansha Castle in 1910 and is interred at Killaldriffe near Kilmoyler.

Give me six foot three, one inch to spare of Irish soil

And dig it anywhere

And for my poor soul say a prayer

Above the spot.

NAPOLEON BONAPARTE

Yes there is a connection between Cahir and the Emperor of France and the King of Sweden.

Carrigatha, on the back road from Cahir to Ardfinnan lived the Clearys, it is said that they had a large amount of land in Cahir and Golden. They were one of the largest landowners in Tipperary. Nothing remains of the great house in Golden as it burned and the stone was used to build houses elsewhere, a branch of the family led by Francis Cleary went to Marseille, France, to seek his fortune and make his fortune he did, he became very wealthy as a Silk manufacturer and Wine merchant. He had a family with a French woman.

Desiree was born in Nov. 1777 and went to the convent school, the French revolution broke her schooling so she was never highly educated..

Being a daughter of a wealthy merchant she travelled in style. Desiree was introduced to the young Napoleon and were engaged, around that time her sister Julie got engaged to Joseph Napoleon. Julie and Joseph were married and their daughter became the Queen of Naples.

Josephine arrived on the scene and the engagement ended. This prompted Desiree to move to Sweden where she married……..Marshal Jean Bapiste Jules Bernadotte…..who became King Charles XIV of Sweden and Desideria [her Swedish name] became his Queen.

The Irish Cleary's continued living in Cahir for a while, The last of them to the late 1980s They kept in touch with their French relations and a bit of cash was always coming from the wealthy cousins. The headstone in Cahir cemetery came from a french sculptor.

Desideria or Desiree passed away in December 1860 and her tomb is to be viewed in Stockholm. A very large oval mound of marble as befitting a Cleary. The name became Clary in France.

When the French monarchy fell, Queen Marie Antoinette was imprisoned for almost 2 years. A manservant Named Francois Clary stayed in her employment, we know nothing about him.

CAHIR MILLS

When the mill opened in 1800 it was by far the largest employer in the town. The Manor Mills was on the bridge across the river from the Castle. Suir Mills was the bakery and Cahir Abbey Mills built in 1775-90. The business was a thriving profitable business managed and run by the Quakers.

250 to 300 families had a wage packet every week, the name changed To Going and Smith mills. They produced the best quality flour and associated products. I remember Balloon Flour. Because our intrepid mothers made bed sheets out of the bags which were made of cotton.

The spin off from the flour business was massive. There were almost 30 licensed premises, all doing well. Draperies, shoe shops, corner shops, shoe menders, a dramatic society and plenty of sports facilities including a boxing club.

Frank Sinatra had a hit with…There's an awful lot of coffee in Brazil ... The local millworkers had their version..There's an awful lot of Coffeys in the mill …

The bombshell dropped in 1965 the mill closed after 150 years, the town saw no future, Meetings were called, I remember Tom Hussey saying that the repercussions would be felt for years..he was right.

THE COALMEN

The most backbreaking job at the time was done by a few hardy men. The Coffeys and the Walls were delivering coal around the town.

Mikey Wall and Billy Wall were renowned fishermen, no salmon ever stood a chance. Both were from the Mountain road. Mikey died a young man and Billy soldiered on for a few years almost crippled from the torture of carrying bags of wet coal into and around peoples houses

A few years before Billy passed away, we were chatting on the bridge. By now he had two walking sticks, the back and legs were giving him trouble. I asked him if he had ever been abroad, he stunned me by saying he was in Alaska. Why Alaska, I asked ?. Would you believe that it was the only place that I had no relations, he said.

CAPTAIN CHRISTY

Scaragh Wood Lodge was hardly the location to breed and train a champion racehorse, It was here that the dream began for Major Joe Pidcock and Mrs Jane Samuel owners of a horse called Captain Christy. Trained by Garret Dooley, Major Pidcock and Pat Taffe. Mossy Casey Snr was with Major Pidcock when the animal was purchased and also helped to train this wonderful horse.

Captain Christy raced 40 times and won 18, among the wins were the Cheltenham Gold Cup..Irish Sweeps Hurdle ... the Scottish Champion Hurdle at Ayr. The Scalp Power Gold Cup at Leopardstown..the King George VI at Kempton. His last season was 1975-1976.

Another Horse that won the Champion Hurdle twice and was bred in Ardfinnan was the great Bula...he had a record of 34 wins out of 51.

Bula was beaten by Captain Christy; he finished fourth behind the Captain in the Leopardstown Sweeps Hurdle.

Both horses broke the track record at different tracks in the 1972-73 season.

BEEKEEPING AND HONEY

Redmond Williams from Tincurry started beekeeping in 1986 and within a few years he had won the World Cup for honey. A quiet and unassuming man who came originally from Carrigeen and is a member of the Cahir Brass Band.

Following his success in London in the World Cup ..at the London Honey Show. He won Gold in 1993 to 1996 was 2nd on three occasions and 3rd twice. With these attributes to his name, he could judge in Ireland, England and Wales and at Kensington in London.

Proficient at AI. in bees and the changing of the temperament in them. He went on the lecture circuit.

This work takes him to neighbouring countries and has been invited to England to lecture on honey and beekeeping.

His work is made more difficult by unscrupulous breeders importing bees with dangerous stings. It is great to have another Gold medallist in the Cahir area.

THE LADY FROM HOGAN SQUARE

Christy Griffin lived in Hogan Square and had one daughter Mary, who went to England in the 60s. Mary secured work as a senior secretary in the British Labour Party and was part of the Harold Wilson Administration. She met and married Harold Walker in 1984. They were married in the Crypt of St. Giles underneath the Houses of Commons. They were the first Catholics to be married there since the reformation in 1526. The Reformation was during Henry VIII's reign.

The Marriage ceremony was celebrated by another Cahir man, the Reverend Peter Cullen of Bengurrah.

Harold Walker was a Minister of State and Deputy Speaker of the house. When he retired in 1997 he became Lord Walker of Doncaster and Mary was dubbed Baroness Walker of Doncaster. Both peerages are for the recipient's lifetime.

Christy Griffin worked as a gardener in the Cahir convent all his life.

HIGH TEA

In the 1960s Cahir House Hotel was considered very upper class and only the wealthy could darken its doors, not many locals were inside to eat or be entertained. Cyril Cusac was passing through town, after all it was the crossroads of the south. The star of stage and screen called to have tea with his lady friend. The pair were seated and the waitress poised to take their order, conscious that she was in the presence of the famous. The star asked for scones and tea, insisting on Indian tea. The waitress apologised and said that the hotel only had Cahir tea.

MOTORING

According to J,Darcy..the best car ever made was the Ford Angela .

SOME PUNISHMENT BY THE BRITISH

Thomas Leamy a native of Cahir, a butcher by trade was tried in Clonmel with stealing a gun...sentenced in April 1827..to seven years transportation to Van Diemen's Land. On the ship ... .Eliza 11.

Patrick Moloney, a shepherd aged 40 was tried in Tipperary with stealing 2 lambs from a man called Donoghue from Cahir. He was sentenced to 7 years transport to Van Diemen's Land, on the ship…. Constant in 1843.

John White tried at Clonmel in March 1831 for the assault on Denis Brien at Kilmoyler ...Sentenced to 7 years transportation..on the Norfolk.

James Carroll, a 40 year old labourer a native of Kilmoyler was charged at Clonmel with stealing sheep. He was sentenced to transportation for life. On the ship… ELIZA 11 in 1827.

Daniel Conrick a native of Toureen in the parish of Kilmoyler. Tried in Clonmel, charged with assaulting and burning the house of Thomas Mc Namara on 28 November 1828 at Toureen…..Hanged in Clonmel the following month.

Edmond Peters, of Kilmoyler aged 17 was charged with larceny in Tipperary Assizes and sentenced to 7 years transportation on the ship, Elphinstone in 1838.

Michael Kearney of Ballingeary Cahir. Charged in Clonmel with larceny and sentenced to 7 years to Van Diemen's Land on the ship, Castle Forbes in 1824…on arrival was to be claimed by a James Carney.

David Byron, a 20 year old labourer from Toureen, tried at Clonmel Assizes. In July 1848, for stealing clothes. Sentence,,, transport for 7 years on the ship ... .Blenheim.

THE SINGER NOT THE SONG

Robbie Martin a well known native of the Cahir district, in the latter days he ran a Milk Business and was known all over south Tipperary. One of his customers was the Cahir Day Care Center. The Center reached a big milestone and invited anyone that was associated with the facility. Being very popular Robbie was high on the list.

On the day he turned up bearing gifts and was welcomed by all, young and the aged. As the night wore on and a few drinks were taken the singing started. Robbie was asked to contribute and being a former member of the Rock Group, Suzy Bullets..he was not versed in the old stuff.

John Lennon's anniversary was that week and Robbie explained that Lennon was shot 30 years before and wrote a song called YESTERDAY…and as a tribute to the former Beatle he would give a rendition. A not so sober man accompanied our boy on the accordion and Robbie gave the worst rendition of all time. When he was finished he heard an old woman say to her friend,,,I think he shot the wrong man.

NED KELLY OUTLAW

Ned Kelly's father, John Kelly was from Moyglass in north Tipperary. he was arrested for selling stolen pigs in the Square of

Cahir. Kelly was sentenced to transportation for 9 years to Van Diemen's Land, now Tasmania. He had a family in Melbourne, It was Ned who became a famous outlaw. The Kelly gang were horse thieves and as time went on they were surrounded and in a shootout, Ned shot Constable Lonergan following a promise from years before…..if I am to ever kill anyone it will be you…Ned was 25 years old when he was hanged at Melbourne Gaol in 1880.

There was an enormous sum of 8,000 pounds on his head that was never paid out. The governor of the prison cut the head off Ned's corpse and displayed the skull as a trophy on his desk for years.

Ned's remains were removed from the Gaol in Melbourne to be finally buried in the town of Greta, Australia in Jan 2013.

DUTCH ELM DISEASE

A Dublin man lovingly called the Nutty Professor lived in Ballymorris with his wife and family for about 30 years. A fair description of him would be a little eccentric. He and his family travelled the world, always to exotic places. As soon as the school holidays were announced, they were off .

On this occasion Peru was the destination and in that country the menfolk do the knitting out of very thick alpaca wool. Our man purchased a very large jumper that reached to his knees and on his return wore this apparel every day.

During their absence the grass was very high and he had to lift up the mower and attack the grass from above…disaster struck he lost his footing and fell back, the mower landing on his chest, but was saved by the heavy wool jumper, the jumper being of such heavy wool caught the cutters and the engine cut out.

Outside his front door was a large Elm Tree that was diseased and needed to be cut down. Our hero enquired of me the cost of a chainsaw.

His wife uttered the best putdown that I have ever heard……She said ..No Mike..anyone that almost cut his throat with a lawn mower ..has no business with a chainsaw…..

TIPPERARY SUPPORTERS

Visiting my old friend Tom Fahey at his home in the magically named Clogheenapishogue….The little stone of the fairy …. Kilcoran. His wife Mary is a GAA fan who attends all the Hurling and Football in the area. Mary would be a Tobin..known all around as a Whitehead. At this time her daughter Orla had announced her engagement to a fellow Garda Where both of them worked in Dublin.

Mary was expecting a visit from her future son in law and was wondering where he was from. I hope he is nice and a GAA man, she was talking to herself while making supper and suddenly she

gasped OMG ... .OMG….OMG…what if he is from Kilkenny?.....
He was from Dublin…..The long suffering husband Tom says ..that
is what I have to put up with.

GARRYCLOGHER N.S 1930
FAMINE TIMES

In the year 1847 and 1848 the potatoes blackened in the ridges
and there was a great scarcity of them. The potatoes grown were
generally called ..The Leather Coats…They were completely wiped
out and it was then ..The Champions, was first grown in the district.

The people got them from Lord Lismore and through the ..Board
Of Guardians ..at Clogheen.

During the Famine many people died of hunger.

Two big strong able men called Glasheen died on the roadside
near Sweeneys Cross. They were said to be the strongest men in the
district. The cause of the Famine was the failure of the potato crop.

It was after the Great Hunger that the Public Works started to
give the poor people work.

Collector James Lonergan [son]

Garryclogher.

The Folklore commission collected these stories in 1930s

CRIMEA BOB

11th Hussars

Underneath

Lies crimea bob

A veteran troophorse

Who after passing unharmed

Through the memorable

Crimean campaign

Died at Cahir barracks

On the 9th november 1862

Aged 34 years

Alma…Balaclava…Inkerman…Sevastopol…

GEOFFREY KEATING

Geoffrey Keating born In Burgess or Moorstown. There are conflicting views, he lived from 1569 to 1644 and is buried at Tubrid, Ballylooby. He was a controversial Catholic Priest and Poet. Among his great works is the History of Ireland from the creation to the arrival of the Normans all written in the irish language. He wrote many books, all are well received by scholars. After obtaining a degree of Doctor of Divinity was appointed to the Parish of Knockgraffon, 2 miles from Cahir. He was popular with the ordinary folk, after stopping the practice of delaying Mass until the local gentry arrived.

In 1990 a monument was raised in the townland of Burgess near the Village of Ballylooby near where he spent some of his life hiding out in caves and writing some of his best work.

SNIPPETS

KEDRA……Cead Rath…….Hundred Forts

Galtee….Gall Tire…..Strangers Land

Garryroan……Garrai Rua…..Red Gardens

Garryclogher…..Garrai Clihe……Stoney Gardens

Knockgraffon…Cnoc Rath Fionn….Hill Fort of John

Kilcommon…. Cill Coman….Comans Church

Sraid na Gcuic……Road Of The Cuckoos

Carrigeen……Little Rock.

Ballydrehid…..The town of the bridge

Poulmucka…..The hole of the pig'

THE PRESIDENTIAL VISIT

The year was 1990 the Labour Party Branch in Cahir was strong with lots of members. It was the Presidential Election year and we in Labour had a strong candidate in Mary Robinson. She was arriving in town to canvas and meet the local Labour branch at the Galtee Hotel. Ernie Alton was the branch Chairman, that meant that nothing was allowed to go wrong. We met for tea and beverages, it was a convivial get together.

Some of the branch held Mary in high esteem almost to the point of veneration.

A presentation was made of a framed print of the Swiss Cottage by our chairman. Mary's husband Nicky asked the reason for the Cottage and before anyone could answer, Jack Doherty said matter of fact…It was a Whorehouse……..a few members almost fainted, whilst the future president laughed out loud and was thankful that there were no reporters about. Jack went on to explain, even though no one was listening, the rumours that the Earl of Glengall, also known as the Foxy Lord, used to take girls from the town into the Cottage for fun and frolics without Lady Margarets knowledge.

Mary Robinson was elected President of Ireland in December 1990 and the print hangs on her wall.

THIRSTY MEN

Times were bad, money was non-existent but the Irish sense of humour was rife. Tom was on the bridge in town one Sunday morning not a penny to his name. It was the time when the Public houses did not open until late on Sunday but some places could be entered by back lanes and such, illegally. Elbows on the bridge gazing into the river Suir waiting for a miracle..

Along comes two American tourists, they stop to look at the weir and ask a question of our Tom. Say buddy, do you know where two thirsty men could get a beer. Tom says that he does not….But he knows where three can.

THE LEGEND OF KNOCKGRAFFON

The story as I heard from many moons ago

Jack Madden was a hunchback, he was walking to town he crossed the river by the ford at Knockgraffon on his way to Cahir. The area was hilly and it was getting dark. He knew that he would not get to town before night. Jack climbed up the Motte and lay down to sleep.

He was awakened by music, such as he had never heard before, and singing sweet voices. He raised his head and he could not believe his eyes. The fairies were holding hands and dancing around a yellow light, singing De Luan, De Mart, De Luan, De Mart, over and over again.

Jack for fun blurted out agus De Satairn the little people stopped at once and tried the new word to their song..De Luan De Mart agus De Satairn and they were delighted because they had been singing the old one for centuries.

Being people with magical powers they asked Jack what he wished for most, Jack said that he could do without his hump. Lo and behold whoosh the lump disappeared and Jack felt 50 years younger.

The following morning he finished his journey to Cahir and Maddens Lane. The locals admired the new Jack and asked how it came to be, he gave them a blow by blow account of what happened.

There was an unpopular man called Will Reilly listening to all this with interest, as he had a hump and it was crippling him.

The next night Reilly made his way to the Motte and bedded down to sleep, early morning he heard the music and hid from the Fairies and blurted out the rest of the week, all seven days in Irish. The little people were confused and not happy…who did that they asked? and Reilly stood and said twas me. The little ones held a meeting to see what was to be done and decided to place Jack Madden's hump upon Reilly's to punish him. Will Reilly did not last very long after that encounter.

Brendan Behan said ..there is no such thing as Fairies…but we Irish know that they are there.

CAHIR POST OFFICE

In 1824 the Post office was in Main St. Probably Castle St. A letter handed in at noon would be in Dublin the next day at 11 o'clock. In 1870 the Post Office was in the Square beside the now Galtee Inn and the Postmaster was Patrick Lonergan. Mrs.Kate Kelly was Postmistress in 1889. This location was in disrepair and there was a question about sanitary arrangements.

Lady Margaret Charteris gave the site for the present office for a nominal amount. There was a delay in commencing the building which caused an outcry in the papers and as far away as the British House of Commons. A Mr Cullinan MP. said in a lively debate that the Unionists were falling asleep on the job.

Eventually Mr Holloway, a builder who had a premises directly across the road from the site, was appointed as the successful bidding contractor. The New Post Office was open for business in 1905 with Mrs Kate Kelly as the Postmistress.

In 1939 an automatic stamp dispenser was installed, with a plea to the public not to use bent coinage. There were several robbery attempts, in Jan. 1922 it was raided by rebels and on 16 Oct. 2013 an attempt to remove the safe involving a large earthmover was unsuccessful.

There was an attempt to downgrade the Office and place it in another location. I am proud to say that I led a campaign to save the Post Office In 2003 An Post wanted to downgrade the premises and sell it off to anyone, as a Labour Councillor it was my job to prevent this happening. Henry Reidy arrived on the scene and saved the day by taking the reins to drive the Post Office forward.

THE FAMINE WINDOW

Down Maddens Lane, The lane that runs beside Morrisons Chemist. There was a window at the rear of Condons Public House that used to help feed the starving populace during The Great Hunger. Condons was the oldest family run pub and restaurant in Cahir before it closed. It has been in business since the 1700s. They also had an Undertaking Business and Photographers studio. Back in the years they had a Travel Agency, with a cardboard cutout of the Titanic.

THE BLOOD DONOR

This story was told to me by Tom himself.

In the days people flocked to give blood a few times a year. The locations were almost always in the National Schools. The donors would turn up to donate a pint of the precious liquid.

Bridie Lonergan was on hand in the old Technical School where she worked. At that time the donor would be offered a cup of tea and biscuits or a small bottle of Guinness.

Tom O Donoghue informed Bridie that he would be along sometime as he never missed a chance to give blood. They both lived in the same neck of the woods and knew each other well.

In Tom's own words..I would turn up about half seven and say my hellos, After I gave my pint of blood I sat down to recover and try a small bottle. Bridie had been stowing them away all afternoon for me and about 9 o'clock the show would be over. I suppose that I am the only one to go and give blood and come out three sheets in the wind. Great auld Times.

GRAVITY

One Christmas eve a great friend of mine was taken all too soon. Noel Haide and myself were sitting at the bar in Lexi Sheehan's pub.

Noel was a very dry wit with a fair capacity for alcohol for a thin man.

The door crashed open, a schoolmate of ours tried to enter the premises while standing up, he failed, and hit the floor like a wet blanket. Noel turns to me and says,,I told ya the gravity is extra strong tonight.

FAMINE

Famine is a useful word when you do not want to use words like Genocide and Extermination.......Frank O'Connor

SONGS PEOPLE SING

In my younger days in the 60s and 70s the pubs were doing as good as they were at any time. These times will never come again.

I can remember the songs that the drinkers sang, each had his own song..Mostly in Coltons pub.

Pat Walsh Ballymacadam......The Mean Rogue.....

I went up the stairs like a good girl should

And the rogue he followed me

Like I knew the rogue he would

He was a mean rogue a bad rogue

A rogue of low degree

And I tell you in a minute the rogue he was a FLEA.

Pearse Fitzgerald

Hauld yer hault sweet marie, you'll never win the Galway plate

for me.

Mattie Martin

Juanita,,,Ita Juanita you're my own sweet love.

Bobby Costigan

Mary Anne Regrets ,,she's unable to see you again, and Big Iron.

Tommy Farrell

Que Sera…when I was just a little boy my mother said to me.

Ned Harris

O Lonesome me…Everybodys going out and having fun…

Jim Harris

Pretty Woman….save your smile for me.

Mick Dempsey

Saint Teresa of the Roses……... .I use the word sing very loosely.

FRIENDS LIKE THIS

Seamus Martin and his wife Pauline were employed by Tipp, FM a Clonmel based local radio station. Seamus had the most listened to spot, 10 to 12, five days a week and Pauline read the news.

It was a week to polling day and my nerves were shot, my chances were good this second time running in the Tipperary South, Local Elections .

Seamus had a piece about the song..A long Way To Tipperary….inviting people to ring in about their thoughts on it. He had it going for a week.

I felt that a minute on the radio would advance my cause and I pulled in the car and rang the station.

I spoke to the researcher and told her that the song was written by Jack Judge. It had nothing whatsoever to do with County Tipperary. It was actually a street in Soho in the West End of London. I have been there many times.

Driving along and waiting for my factual account to be broadcast all over Tipperary, the moment arrived.

Seamus tells the country that he has another view on the song, he says that Seanie Lonergan the Labour Candidate rang in to say. that it is a Whore House in Soho and if anyone would know he would.

Pauline says… he'll kill you, it's a good job that he is not drinking. All our Seamus says is that there is no such thing as bad publicity…..I recovered and was successful in the election. We are still friends.

WATERING HOLES

In Cahir as a teenager I had a big choice of pubs to be thrown out of in 1967

Irwin's Galtee Inn, Mrs.Murphy's, Franklin's Condons, John Burkes Stop Inn, Caplices, Galtee Hotel, Mulcahys, Jack Ryans Cahir House Hotel, Butlers Josie Wyse, Phil Boyles Sunderlands, Bridge Bar, Ned Ryans, Coltons, Black Tom's, Morrisseys, Cuck Hennessey's, Crokes, Noel Fitzgerald.

The choice is limited with only seven watering holes now. 2024. Hill Inn, 22 Abbey St. Morrisseys Shamrock Inn, Galtee Inn. Punters Rest and Cahir House Hotel. That's Progress.

DARKEST DAY

I remember being in school that day. When the Guard came in and called for Michael Kelly..saying that he was needed at home, Later that evening the story unfolded. It was 1st February 1960.

Little Mary Sunderland was playing with her ball on Blind St. when the ball rolled down the slip beside the forge into the river. 3 year old Mary followed the ball down to the river and went too far in, the current caught her and she was powerless. Michaels father Paddy Kelly worked in the Cahir Mills and saw what happened. The river was in flood and Paddy shouted for help and jumped in. Normally he was a strong swimmer and on this occasion he caught hold of Mary and held her up for a millworker to grab her.

In the river near the eye of the bridge the current formed a whirlpool and Paddy struck his head on the bridge arch and lost his grip on Mary.

The flooded river carried them both off and both Paddy and Mary perished together. It was Cahirs Darkest day.

Greater love hath no man, than he who lay down his life for his friend.

OLD ROAD

John Butler of Ballymacadam owned a horse that everyone in the horsey circles envied. He was the proud owner of a bay Eventer bought at Goresbridge as a 3 year old called Old Road. This was no ordinary equine and was not without his little idiosyncrasies, for instance he would not let you wash his ears with cold water, it had to be lukewarm. He was terrified of pigs. Apart from Eventing in Ireland. Among his travels abroad brought him to compete in England at Badminton 3 times as well as European Championships 3 times and the World Equestrian games in Aachen in Germany and Fountainbleu in France

Michael Ryan returned from Switzerland to take on training Old Road. He retired in May 2012.

The brilliant horse passed away at the age of 24 years.

PICKING THE WHORTS

To us they were called Hurts their proper name was Whortleberries and sold now from overseas as Blueberries. Everybody in town in summer headed for the mountains above Cahir with their buckets and gallon tins, sandwiches and cold tea. This was the 60s

It was hard earned small money but small was better than none.

You walked early in the morning to stake your claim, trying to avoid places where the midges and the horse flies would not get you. The most terrifying was the Horse fly; he had a bite like poison.

Apart from the flies the summers seemed to have been hotter and sunburn was a big risk. Scrapes from falling and bushes were a hazard.

If you were lucky to have your containers full at evening, you made your way down to the wood gates. There Timmy Looney or Willie Hickey were waiting to weigh and pay you a few pence for your gatherings.

Grubs of Castlegrace used to buy the berries as well as Elderflower and Elderberries and Blackberries, the latter were the worst because of the briars. This went on for many years and thank God it is only a memory.

RABBITS

Another activity that went well into our adulthood was lamping rabbits. For years Jerry Donoghue and myself would be out all night catching our dinner. We did not go in for setting snares like a lot of our contemporaries, we always had a dog and the lamp.

Lots of families lived on rabbits, Nell Haide who fed me more than once used to stuff and roast the rabbit and it was fantastic, whereas Bridie Lonergan always made stew. When I moved out into the world I made rabbit curry that lasted all week, that and wild deer meat..venison.

The lamp was a headlight from a motorbike, the motorbike battery was nice and light in a school bag on your back.

The best dog we ever had was Trooper, we would dazzle the rabbit and Trooper would nab him.

During the Second World War rabbits were in great demand, they used to be exported to England as well as the Irish cities. A man called Pork Pie Griffin became a millionaire sending to England rabbit meat in pies.

LONG EARS

A few years after moving to Garryroan my beloved and I were in discussion about the garden. She actually wanted me to go digging a plot to plant potatoes. I informed her that I was a townie and we were not cut out for that. She said that I was very good at picking them from the plate, I could not deny that

The discussion was in full flow when a traveller man pulled up outside the wall. Behind the car was a flat trailer carrying a donkey tied to an upright on the trailer.

Elbow out the window he shouted in …would you buy an ass sir?

Before I had time to answer, my beloved shouted back at him..I already have one..

LAWRIE WILLIAMSON

As can be worked out by the name he was not born in Cahir but he lived for a long time among us, he and his wife Gill.

Lawrie was Scottish and Gill was half Irish; she was a Butler. They were both very good artists, Lawrie commanded big money for his work

They built a fantastic house in Knockgraffon and lived a happy life.

I was friendly with them and visited them a lot. We had Bantam hens and Lawrie loved the eggs. Lawrie was well in his 80s and his health was failing. but he still worked at his art.

One day in 2018 as I called, he beckoned me into the kitchen and pointed to the faucet or kitchen sink tap and said that it had been replaced at a cost of 70 euro……..That's what I gave for my first house he said. Lawrie's and Gill's ashes were emptied in the river Derwent.

BOMBERS

Another Mr. Darcy ism, in the early 2000s, we were discussing terrorism. He came out with the classic,,,Those suicide bombers must be on big money.

AMERICAN EMBASSY

You could not make this up, this is fact 2004 and Johnny D. decided he would travel a bit so he packed his bags and went to Germany with a pal of his. They found work in an abattoir boning meat. Things were going all right for a long time and the friend said that he had enough and went off leaving Johnny on his own.

In his own words our John said that he would go to the other end of Germany….Amsterdam, things might be better there.

Is the reader beginning to get the picture?

In Holland's capital city Johnny was mugged and everything was taken except his phone, because had it in his pants. No money, no clothes and nothing to eat, he called home and asked his mother to send money. His poor mother was beside herself with worry, because she knew that Johnny was no academic.

Johnny made it home and I met him after a few days and asked how he got on.This day last week I had my dinner in the American Embassy, says John. Naturally I enquired what he was doing in the American Embassy…..He said my mother was sending me money, Curious, I asked again and got the same answer. There was a huge crowd at the front door so I went to the back. These are Johnny's words ... .A big black soldier in a helmet answered the door and asked Johnny what he wanted. Our boy said the mother sent money and that he had nothing to eat for days. The Marine brought him in and gave him dinner and sorted Johnny out.

It took a short while to figure out that our Johnny should have been looking for the American Express Office.

THE BLAME GAME

Col.Murdock was collecting a high load in a car trailer, when a worker at the railway tied it for him, only to tie it through the spokes of the wheel. Murdock said,,,I do not blame that man….I blame his parents.

THE LONERGANS

We were happily ensconced up around Lough Derg from ancient times When the Anglo Norman Butlers drove us down south to Cahir and Cashel.

Castlegrace was our Family seat and castle. The Battle of Clontarf saw King Lonergan excel himself at fighting, in 1014.

Later From the 12th to 15th centuries we supplied the church with Bishops and Archbishops and many lesser ecclasiastics as well as supplying Harpists to the Irish Clan Leaders.

Donat O Lonergan was Archbishop of Cashel in 1152.

Anne Lonergan was an Irish Nun imprisoned during the French Revolution.

John Lonergan from Toureen was Governor of Mountjoy Prison.

O' SULLIVANS

Every O'Sullivan that ever was, came from Knockgraffon just outside Cahir. The O Sullivan's land extended to Carrick-On-Suir and all lands in between. The Normans deprived the Clan of their lands and sent them to the Mountains of Cork and Kerry. The O'Sullivan's split into two clans. The O 'Sullivan Mor and O'Sullivan Beare .

All is well again. A wealthy American man called O'Sullivan purchased the Motte of Knockgraffon and has it back in the clan name after all these years.

O 'Sullivan who delights not in violence

Rules over the extensive Eoghanacht of Munster

About Knockgraffon he obtained his lands

After the victory of conflicts and battles.

THE TECHNICAL SCHOOL

This story was told to me the night my mother Bridie Lonergan was in the funeral home. By John Mackey a teacher in the Tech.

He begins…twas the week that John Wayne won the Oscar…Bridie was sweeping the hallway. Jim Flanagan, an absolute gentleman and school principal was getting a mouthful from an irate parent, from a woman that thought her child was entitled to special treatment.

She really lost it, she was screaming abuse and insulting all the staff. Jim was trying to pacify her by edging her to the front door. After what seemed an age he successfully had her outside, He promised her that she would get her way, if she would calm down..she did.

Jim turned to go back to his office and as he passed Bridie she said, Know what Jim, they gave the wrong man the Oscar.

JOHNNY O' BRIEN

Another story that Johnny told me many years ago.

One of Johnny's earliest memories was about 1913, sitting at his mothers feet in the house on the Mountain Road. His baby brother died the previous day. His mother had the infant wrapped in a blanket. John remembered digging a hole in the clay floor with a spoon. His mother kept patting in back in place with her foot

His mother and father with four surviving siblings were waiting for the neighbours to arrive near midnight with spades and lanterns, to inter the little body.

The belief and superstition at that time is that the Fairies would take the boy if he was buried before midnight.

The sombre procession with their lanterns made their way to the Old Abbey just off Abbey Street. The infant was interred. There Was no priest in attendance, the little party of mourners said their own prayers. Johnny's relationship with the Church was not a very good one.

LINEN AND STRAW

A linen factory was established in Cahir under the Cahir local association in 1809, [The year that Willie Brennan was hanged. Also the year that the last person to die by Ducking Stool her name was Jenny Pipes her crime was for being a Common Scold] This laid the foundation of a spinning school; and in 1823 a market was established for the sale of linen and yarn In 1829 the Earl and Countess of Glengall established a fancy straw plait manufacture and the products gained a medal from the Society of Arts. It employed a large number of females.....In 1823 the Earl gave more funds and it was then enabled to carry on ....In 1837 it employed 68 girls and arrangements were made for expansion, The plaited straw and fine linen was very well received in the foreign fashion circles as it was made into mens and womens sun hats and fans and so on.

Cahir town population in 1831 was 3408 and the parish was…8594 whilst in 1841 the town was 3668 and the parish was 8801.

In 1834 there were 8,507 Catholics and 70 dissenters.

The Fever hospital also known as Kennedy's hospital had 220 patients in 1839. The famine was still a short few years away.

Jackson, a quaker of Millgrove, was building a flax mill at Brookfield, a short distance from his home.[flax is the raw material for linen].The flax plant was grown in all the neighbouring townlands and the large soaking ponds were near the children's famine house.

Millgrove was on the old road to Cork and horses and carts were the mode of transport at the time. Being a resourceful man Jackson had a watering station for people and horses. Bianconi type stages were constantly on the road.

Were you to go to Millgrove now you would travel over an old bridge, but look under and you will see that the stream has disappeared, in its heyday the stream used to run a millwheel such was the amount of water there. The Quakers had a small flour mill there hence the name Millgrove. It is said that the Quakers built the railway from Limerick Junction to Rosslare and paid for it themselves.

The Quakers proper title is The Society of Friends.

MORRISSEY'S PUB

Mrs. Morrissey had a pub, restaurant and bed and breakfast in Castle Street and did a thriving business because she was so popular. In 1980 a film called Excalibur was partly made in the Castle across the road. The crew and some of the actors stayed in the pub. They all

wanted to stay, the owner said that she did not have enough beds for them all. They went and bought their own beds and squeezed them into the rooms. The sing songs lasted long into the nights.

Richard Burton and Trevor Howard at another time frequented the Pub.

All the fishermen used to drink and have their meetings there, some great characters and great fishermen.

One evening the owner's son James went fishing with Tommy Farrell also known as ..The Puck. And on their return they entered the pub having a few words, it seems that James was casting out and the hook caught Tommy in the lobe of the ear, the hook was well embedded, plans were put in place for the removal of the hook, someone got a pliers and the victim was put lying on the long seat, while two weighty men sat on Tommy. Mag Lillis the barmaid was given the job of cutting the hook and extracting the offending piece of metal forwards out of our boy's ear. To say that the air turned blue with the swearing and threats against the people holding him down would be an understatement. Several whiskeys later all was back to normal. Another time Mrs Morrissey put a beef joint into the oven in the kitchen. The cooker was run by bottle gas. The gas ran out as Mag Lillis was putting on the kettle to make a cup of tea. She changed the gas bottle and went back to the bar, unaware of the beef in the oven…..The old woman was halfway down the hall when it exploded, she was lifted off her feet and slammed against the front door, she survived shaken and still alive. The kitchen however had to be completely outfitted

The whole building shook. They had a dog named Guinness, that was deaf as a stone following the incident Following Mrs Morrissey's passing.. The pub was first prize in a raffle put up by Guinness Ltd. This was a novelty at the time and a brilliant advertising opportunity in the States. It is not divulged the amount of tickets that were sold .

The winners were a couple from Milwaukee, Doug and Suzanne Knight. Doug was a sound engineer and was somewhat musical, he wrote a song about Cahir and it is still played online.

Brian Costigan is the present owner in 2024 and has left the Morrissey name over the pub.

THE RIVER SUIR

This account of the Suir from 1887 tells us that the river above the Castle bridge was utilised for boating purposes, by about a dozen private owners. Annually in September a regatta and athletic sports are held. This year the prize money averaged at about 40 pounds. The Mall, a walk along the river, shaded by lime, beech and horse chestnut trees is the starting point. It is still the same today.........We are told that the river running through the estate is strictly preserved. Lady Mag. would like us to go to the Aherlow where there is good trout fishing.

Cahir Park House commands a delightful view of the river running through a park of 560 acres. We are told that Lady Margaret is a regular visitor to her lovely Swiss Cottage. But not it seems as regular as the Foxy Lord himself. The river was well known all over the country as well as abroad for its Trout and Salmon fishing. The wealthy purchased long tracts of the river for very large sums of money. The Suir is the engine for a lot of mills along its banks, it drives several mills in Cahir and down river to Ardfinnan and so on as it wanders its way to the sea at Waterford.

Before the mill at Cahir and before the weir was built...[the weir was engineered to direct water towards the mill, to turn mill wheels and later turbines] The river was navigable and there are pencil drawings of barges being towed by horses. In the old bakery on the

Cashel road there is a great example of an old mill wheel run by the river.

I remember days of old when fishermen came home with baskets full of trout and anglers with salmon and pike, will we ever see it again?

A NIGHT AT THE OPERA

It is not often that a talent like Jennifer Davis comes along, those that follow opera will have heard and loved this young woman's voice.The Royal Opera House in London is where Jenny came through the Royal Opera House Young Artist Program. As the name suggests the Opera House is patronised by Royalty, on this occasion Prince Charles was in attendance and heard Jennifer sing, He then invited her to sing at his birthday party. In the middle of April 2024, Jenny has just returned from Copenhagen and has performed in America, Slovakia, she has been to Germany many times following her triumphal lead in Wagner's Lohengrin in Germany's capital Berlin.

She has performed in many Scandinavian operas and locally the Great hall in Cahir castle, Cashel and Wexford opera festival. There is hardly a county in Ireland that Jenny has not performed. A soprano that will soon be on the world stage we salute her. Her mother

Maggie is a music teacher and her father Brendan a retired sound engineer.

BEYOND THE PYRAMIDS

1999 saw the arrival of the first Egyptian refugees, who were led by Nagi Barsoum and Thavait Mina. They were escaping persecution in Alexandria and Cairo as Christians by the Muslim majority. They found work almost immediately in the Beef Plant. All the arrivals were very religious and were Coptic Christians, their own Priests came with them and the priests organised all of the congregation. They purchased a building on the Priests Road to worship in 2004. As time went by they settled in and made themselves permanent. In 2013 they purchased the disused Convent and held their worship there. Before the faithful had a permanent location to practise their faith, the sisters allowed the use of the convent. The only difference in their beliefs is that they have their own Pope. In his innocence the Coptic priest invited me to mass on Sunday. I declined because their Sunday mass lasts for 5 hours.

WHO WOULD BE A POLITICIAN

During my time as an elected member of the South Tipperary Council from 2004 to 2014. I had some unusual requests.

Late one night I had a phone call from a constituent, a little bit under the weather. It seems that he had met a married woman that night and he intended to move in with her, the problem was the husband. He wanted me to inform the man that ..and I quote..That his wife was now off the menu and she belonged to him. I declined to do this, his opinion of me changed somewhat….. Several days later he went to Dublin

I held a clinic in the market yard for some time and had a strange mix. A man in his 40s came to me with a problem. I asked where he worked and he said…Work doesn't suit me.

It was nearing back to school time when a mother approached me to get help to pay for the children's school books. While I was taking the details I asked how her summer went…..she said it was brilliant because she was just back from a month in the BAHAMAS and it was just fab.

Phone call on Christmas Day. Sorry to bother you on Christmas Day, could you get me the forms for the grant. I forgot to mention it the last time we met. I didn't want to bother Councillor Marie Murphy.

I always vote for you DAN. Said to me during an election.

I think that you are the best man in the Council. I always vote for you. I never miss an election. I need a favour done……Jaw drops when I tell him that I am out of the Council for 10 years.

The Cahir Labour branch had a Christmas ..ton of coal..draw for years. I wore a Labour badge and the Labour party was on the tickets. I knocked on the door and asked if she could buy a ticket and support us. She says, of course I will, give me a book. I always support Labour because Sean Sampson got me this house……………..Sean Sampson was FINE GAEL.

AN ENGLISHWOMAN IN CAHIR

In the 1960s I worked for a vet called Colm Flynn who had a very busy practice. One of his customers was a small Englishwoman called Miss Armitage. This woman had a homestead on the Khyber or Ballydrehid. She came from England before the second world war. England was under siege from Germany and some friends of hers were killed in the bombing, leaving two children orphaned. This little woman who was unmarried went to London and adopted the two orphans and brought them to Cahir she reared them to adulthood.

Her passion was for pigs and she had many unusual breeds, she was the first person to Import Landrace boars and sows into Ireland. The breed was an enormous success. To say that she was popular would be an understatement, everyone loved this gentle woman. I remember a man called Joe Nolan worked for her.

OLD MILES

At the entrance to Garryroan House to the left of the gate is a rare mile stone, with 93 carved into it. This road of course would be the old Cork -Dublin road in times gone by. 93 Irish miles, not statute or kilometres. Dublin is 130 statute miles from this spot. The British army barracks was on this road at Kilcommon. The Earl of Cardigan and his troops and cavalry would have used this on their way to Fermoy. The hanging tree was at the Whitechurch cross. It has only recently been taken away. It had gone past its prime. The tree had been there for hundreds of years. Children on their way to school had carved their names into the bark. Adults that were courting carved their lovers' names. Folklore has it that there were 12 men hanged from it .

When the dead tree was removed a few years ago, Denis and Lorraine Slattery pressured the Council to have a replacement tree of the same kind [Beech] put in its place. A fine specimen now stands there.

DAN AND THE BOAR

Characters like this don't come around too often.

A mile outside town on the Cork road lived a man called Dan Hart. Dan kept boars because at that time people brought the sows to the boar. Michael O Neill and myself were asked to mend a few slates on the roof of Dan's house. We were there for about an hour when Dan shouted tea. While we were having the tea made by Dan's wife. Dan told us that he was heading for a serious operation, his wife said will you shut up, it's a thing of nothing. D'ya hear her, she was at me all the other day like that.

I couldn't stand it any more so I went down to Billy the boar. I told Billy that I was heading for a cataract operation. Billy put his head on my lap and listened to me. You see he is a great friend. I told him of the risks involved and the terrible danger that I might not make it, I could die on the table, I could be blind if it did not go alright. I would have to spend the rest of my days in the poorhouse……..I looked down and the tears were streaming down Billy's face…..

STEVE THE KERRYMAN

Steve used to drink in Sean Irwin's pub and was always on the lookout for an unsuspecting victim. Most of his stories were long and convincing until the last line. He would gauge his victim and if he was a sportsman, he was in. Steve was playing for Kerry, there was never anyone like him. In the rare time that Kerry would be doing bad. Steve would be called to take them out of trouble. Twas getting near half time and steve wanted to get a goal or two before they went for the oranges. It is according to Steve awhile since Con Houlihan said of me, that man is the best fielder of a ball that ever lived…….Modesty was not a barrier…Steve went up for a ball just as the ref blew for the break, he looked at his watch and shouted Steve you can come down now.

Countless people up through the years had to listen to that.

THE MOVING STATUE

I think it was around 2010 that vandals struck at the Holy Well in Cahir. In Tiobar Iosa all the statues were destroyed, so I was approached to do something about it. The main statue was The Sacred Heart lifesize. A very tall order. In my search I hit paydirt. A friend of mine, a Cleric, knew where there was one and it was not being used.

He informs me that the people of Clogheen might not like the idea of the statue leaving the parish. Listen I said it is going to be put to good use and it will be prayed for every day.

OK but you will have to come in the dark of night because I don't want you to be seen. This is solid and it is very heavy so bring help.

I ring the help Jerry Niland…..howya Jer I need a lift…will do it tomorrow…no it has to be done at night…..piss off … .it's all legal and above board….yeah sounds like it.

After a long time he agrees, we hit off with the trailer and extra help Waylon and Emmet my sons and Marjorie.

Nine o clock of a winters night we struggle to get it out, grunting this is a ton weight ..we have it in the trailer and off we go.

Waylon made a house for the statue to protect it from the elements.

We prepared a site at the well for it……..The call came from the Cleric,….Seanie they missed it and want it back….you have to bring it back they are talking about getting the law involved.

Jerry…..need help tonight keep everything under wraps….Jer says I knew that this would end badly…same deal dark hush hush.

Jerry says that if he is asked how he got the weekend he can't tell them I can't even tell my wife, she would kill me for robbing the church …I say we are furthering the cause of the church by putting this at the Well. You tell her that ... No. At the church the Cleric wants it in the middle of the aisle on a pedestal. His plan is that when the people come ..he will shout a miracle the holy effigy has returned. Oh for a quiet life.

This might sound like a tall story but it is very true.

HOLY WELLS

Some of these wells may be a little outside the Cahir area, we will mention all of them. Tobar Iosa we have covered a few times.

St Kierans Ballylooby Tubrid, St Malachy's Clogheen

Navauns Brown Bog, Pecauns Toureen, St Berriherts Ardan, Sean Shepeil, Newcastle.

The legend of Kieran's Well in Tubrid Ballylooby.

St Patrick came to Ireland in the year 432 and some time after that He needed to have a meeting with St Declan and St Kieran to discuss boundary problems. St Kieran was residing in Tubrid, so he arranged to have their meeting there. The three met and an argument ensued. While the negotiations were in full flow, a pregnant woman was passing and saw the three holy men arguing .

The woman went into labour and was in difficulty but the three were on hand to help. We need salt, said one and St Declan put out his hand with a fistful of salt. Now we need water, St Patrick struck the ground with his staff and a fresh water well appeared. The three holy men delivered the child and all was well and that is how the Holy Well is there.

ST MALACHY'S CLOGHEEN

The grounds of Shanbally Castle is the location of St Malachy's Holy Well. The story that I learned is of two of the ladies of the castle who used the well frequently and were very devout. One of the girls commissioned a solid silver cross to be erected at the well. This was done amid great fanfare, and the following day it had disappeared, they were shocked. Who would do such a thing? They cried.

Another story is that the staff began doing the washing of clothes in the well and were punished by the Saint, after a time the well went dry. It has flowing water only on special times. The location is magical, beneath a canopy of yew trees that completely cover the Well like a roof.

HOGAN THE REBEL

Sean Hogan was one of the leaders of the 3rd Tipperary Brigade. One of the actions that set off the war of Independence was the ambush and shooting dead of two RIC men who were escorting a load of gelignite to a quarry. Sean Treacy..Dan Breen and Sean Hogan went on the run with an increased reward of 10,000 pounds on each of their heads. They were the cause of getting all of South Tipperary placed under Martial Law. Sean Hogan married Christina Butler of Millgrove House in Rathmines Church, Dublin on the 24 Feb.1925...He died in 1968 and is interred in St Michael's Cemetery, Tipperary town.

BATTLE OF BRITAIN

The Battle of Britain was from 10th July 1940 until 31st Oct. 1940. It was between these two dates that Paddy Walsh of the Mall, got a lift from some neighbours to Tramore for the day.

The battle was mostly fought over the English Channel, but on this day Paddy and the people of Tramore were witnessing a pair of Fighter Planes weaving and shooting at each other. They had broken away from the battle proper. Flying at speeds in excess of 300 miles an hour it did not take long to reach the Irish Coast. The German plane was hit and crash landed on Tramore strand. Paddy, like all of the children, ran to where it landed, the pilot was still alive and was arrested by the Gardai.

Told to me by Paddy Walsh.

CLASH NA MBAN

In Husseystown, a very quiet road.....The gathering of the women....... is the literal translation......It is believed that in the time of the British Garrison in Cahir and Clonmel that the Soldiers and others would meet the women there. The women were already on the road, they came from nearby towns. We are to believe that the couples would walk hand in hand along the road. The name would give one food for thought.

THE SHEEP STEALERS

At the side of a bohreen in Mortlestown, was a family named Scanlon. In the year 1848 people were minding their livestock at night. Those that had sheep had to pay special attention because there was a big run on sheep stealing around the area. The neighbours would club together to mind the sheep and there was a flock of 28 sheep belonging to one of the neighbours, and all of a sudden he counted 29 and then 30. He waited for a break in the cloud and caught two men dressed in white sheets stealing the sheep. He made a rush through the flock and captured the two fellows. Who were they but their neighbours ..the Scanlons. They reported them to the Cahir militia and they were brought to the Courthouse and then across the bridge to the Bridewell. Probably Carrigeen Castle.

A search was done on their farm and between two haystacks was an underground passage leading to a butchers shop and slaughterhouse where they prepared the carcases for market

They would take the meat to a butcher in Clonmel on the Narrow Street. that would take the carcasses from them and sell it over the counter.

The sentence handed down was transportation for life to Van Diemen's Land. The pair were brought to Queenstown and put aboard ship and never heard of again.

In the Rose of Tralee Festival of 1976, an Australian girl representing Melbourne was interviewed and her name was Scanlon, she said that she had Irish descendants that were deported for Sheep Stealing and that they came from Tipperary.

Ger. O' Brien from the Tipperary Road made every attempt to make contact with her but to no avail ... .On Liam Tierney's land today there are two fields called Scanlons Fields. This may confirm that there were Scanlons living in that area in the 1800s.

KNOCKAGH HILL

There was a Sub King on his way to Derrygrath to pay special tribute to a Chieftain in that area. On his way back he was slain on Knockagh Hill. A tall slim stone was erected in his memory on Knockmorris Hill.

FAIR DAYS
GER O' BRIEN

Before the Cattle Mart was built in Cahir in 1955 the farmers would take over the town, it would be taken over for the day by the farmers and cattle buyers. Shops would have put up barricades to protect their windows. Many of the brackets are still in place. On the older buildings the railing hooks can still be seen. The animals would occupy one side of the bridge and you had to walk the gauntlet of cow dung on your way to school. Generally the farmers from Ballingeary side would keep their animals on Church St. or the Square. The farmers always kept to their own side of town. The animals had to be in place before 7.30 so it was a big job to hunt them several miles. For the first mile the beasts would be very frisky but after a mile or two he would calm down. It was probably that they were tired, that they stood on one spot for the day and were not corralled in.

Failure to sell meant that the animals were returned home, and animals that were sold for export were hunted across to the railway siding beside the Presbyterian Church on Abbey Street.

The sheep fair took place on Barrack Street and the high path on the Cork road.

There was only one fair per month in Cahir and some farmers would hunt the cattle to town the night before and keep them in a field close by.

The fair day was the day that all the businesses did very well.

THE CURSE OF CROMWELL

Cromwell departed Cahir after the surrender and set his eyes on Fethard. His route took in the priests' road and passed Ballingeary. It had to be some sight because it took him a week to reach Fethard.

He travelled on to Black Bawn Bog and he sank, it took him days to pull the heavy guns out of the mire. He laid siege to Fethard and sent his son in law Ireton to Cashel. Worse than Cromwell had to come in the shape of the Plague, it was spreading rapidly through the populace. Most of the surviving Irish were transported across the Shannon to Connaught and the lands were planted with Cromwellian settlers

CHANGING TIMES

Where the Aldi supermarket now stands on Lower Abbey St. used to be a concrete block yard. For years Paddy Devereux had a blockyard and a sand and gravel business there.

Before that however in the 50s and 60s it was the site of the town dump, where all the household waste was taken to. At that time very little was thrown away and almost everything was recycled. There was no such thing as huge trucks collecting the bins. The County Council had a few horses and carts doing the collection.

Three of the last men that I remember with Council horses were Willie Meagher of Kilcoran and Gerry Cleary from Kilcommon, and of course Jimmy English.

BLIND STREET

It goes under Lower Abbey St. now. The old folk called it Blind St. because at one time there was a wall running across the road on the Tipperary side. There were ruins of houses to the left at the top, known as the rocks. Almost all the time sitting there was a traveller woman called Lizzie the Fluther who was always under a black shawl smoking a stub of a tobacco pipe.

A very unique design of a forge was built in 1902 by the Charteris estate. Beside the forge there was a slope down to the river that was used to water animals that were on the move. All animals were hunted or driven to their destination by road. Cattle and sheep were managed by Drovers for long drives.

The last blacksmith to work the forge was Ned O'Brien of Avondale Court. The age of the Horse dwindled away and Ned turned his hand to metal engineering until his retirement.

A rather unique business was started in the forge by Costigan Undertakers. It is a funeral home now where the deceased spend their last night. This business guarantees that the wonderful structure will carry on and not be fodder for developers.

RIDDLES FROM 100 YEARS AGO

Why is Castle Street dangerous?

Because there is a Wolf there…………….Mattie Wolfe Jeweller.

Why is Mountain road posh?

Because there are Kings on it……………Mr.and Mrs King.

Why is Market St. Poor?

Because they only have a few halfpennys…………Mr.and Mrs Hpenny.

How is it always summer on the Mountain Road?

Because the Swallows live there………….Mr and Mrs,Danny Swallow.

Why did the chicken pick the pot?.

Because he could not lick it.

What fruit will you see on a penny?

A date.

Did Good Friday ever fall on Easter Monday?

Yes, a horse named Good Friday fell in the Grand National.

What is the difference between a train driver and a Teacher?

One trains the mind the other minds the trains.

What is the difference between a Jailer and a Jeweller?.

One sells watches and the other watches the cells.

A man goes to the Doctor with a spear all the way through him.

Doctor…does it hurt?

Patient…only when I laugh.

What is black and white and red all over?.

A Newspaper…………read.

FORGES IN THE TOWN

Dan Guirey Clonmore.Cahir 1930.

There were four forges in Cahir in the late 1890s. Reidys...Leahys..Burkes and O Dwyers. All were in the town except O Dwyers which was at the crossroad on the Mitchelstown road. It was demolished recently. All the buildings have horseshoe shaped doors but only one has a fireplace. They all use hammer and anvil, pincers and rasps and turn out all sorts of implements like colters and socks for ploughs. O Dwyer usually works in the open air when wheel banding. The old folk say that blacksmiths have a cure for rickets. The best place to meet people and catch up on all the news is the Forges.

There used to be an old forge near Whitechurch graveyard belonging to the Reidys for generations. This forge was famous for the quality of work. People came from far and wide to this great blacksmith. They say that Reidy shod Cromwell's horse as he was ransacking Garryroan house and lands. Reidys also made the pikes for the fenians before the Rising at Ballingarry. It is said that the Blacksmiths that were first tenants of the forge in Blind St were descendants of these Reidys.

On the main drag out of town on the Clonmel road is Burkes forge, a slated building with a large door. The forge has two fires one behind the other, with a pair of huge bellows Mr. Burke does all the work on the anvil. The smith shoes horses and donkeys and makes gates, ploughs and harrows.

Mr Burke's father and brother are carpenters and that is handy to combine the two trades making carts, drays and wheels. Mr Burke's decision to become a smith was a wise one. As a rule a smith shoes horses in the open air and has to have a large amount of water from the pump. There is an old saying that the smith has a cure for warts, You cure them by putting the offending limb into the water that the smith uses to cool the shoes.

Dan Guirey ends up saying that this blacksmith is very honest.

The Burkes are still going on the Clonmel road. In 2024

THE WAKE

The funerals around Ballingeary and Mortlestown were considered events of stamina. You would not go to a wake at all in the 19th century unless there were 10 Jars, each one containing a gallon of whiskey for the people that attended. Snuff was given out freely and when they got a bit merry, they would give up the crying about the funeral and start singing songs. Before long they would be dancing out in the yard, it was really a celebration of the life of the person that died. If it was the funeral of a young person there would be no dancing or singing, only the whiskey. There was a distillery in Cahir and the whiskey was purchased there at 2 shillings and sixpence per Jar, so it was affordable.

Old man Shortiss died in Ballingeary west when he was in his 90s. The neighbours and surviving family were very drunk at the wake and set about burying the old man. After the burial they had more whiskey and celebrated well into the night. Next day they came down stairs and old man Shortiss was still in the corner…..there was another night ahead.

PLACE NAMES

On the farm of a man Named Sheehan in the townland of Roosca. There is a rock in a field called the Mass Rock, Because Geoffrey Keating used to say Mass there.

Poulmucka got its name because a pig fell into a very deep hole there.

In Kilcommon there is a field owned by Mr. Ahearne that is called the long field, Because it is so long that they used to course horses there before the races.

Lochloher got its name from a St Luachir that was building a house there but he had no water, so he dug a well hence Loch Luachair.

In Kilcommon, Loch Eibhlis ….a woman of this name used the well.

LANDLORDS

About 1881 around the time of the land war, many families in Ballymacadam were to be evicted from their lands and houses.

Edmund Walsh who resides there, had combined with his neighbours. Not to pay the rent to the landlord. The English soldiers were coming to carry out the eviction.

But James O Mara, the father of Pat O Mara who now owns the land, had a terrible fear of the soldiers, so he had paid the rent, unknown to Edmond Walshe and the others.

The Sheriff and the soldiers came to Walshe's and all the neighbours were there with pitchforks and sticks and stones. The women were armed with bad eggs. A fierce fight broke out between the soldiers and the people of Ballymacadam. The skirmish lasted about an hour and in the end it was the soldiers that took flight. A woman of the Walshe's was so upset that she died after a short time.

Told By Eileen McEniry. Ballyhennebry. 1930

CARRIGEEN COTTAGES

A brand new housing estate in 1939, the people that moved in thought that they were in luxury, even though there was no running water, no inside toilets or electricity. It would be another 15 years before electricity was installed in1954.

One of the house owners, John Lonergan, a postman, had an aunt that went to America, her name was Margaret Duggan and she became George Bernard Shaw's cook. When she retired she returned to Cahir, she lived in Sraid Na Gcuic until she passed away in 1958.

Albert Pierrepoint hanged almost 600 people, he was the official hangman for the British Isles and Ireland. His father Henry and his uncle Thomas were official hangmen before him. His 25 year career ended in 1956. His housekeeper however was a Mrs Hennessy nee Quinlan that came from Kilcoran, Cahir. She remained in England when she retired.

THE POST TRAIN

Back in the day when people wrote letters, the postal service was in great demand. In Cahir railway station there was a sub post office. The trains were travelling sorting offices. The trains and the post worked hand in hand. In the station you could post letters and parcels and buy stamps. You were charged 1 penny, a late fee, if you were not on time. Several members of the postal workers were proficient in Morse Code namely Ernie Alton and Johnny Casey. Cahir Post Office was one of the first to have a telephone exchange. Evelyn O Connell and Mrs Burke of the Railway Bar were the best at Morse for Telegrams.

UNION

In Barrack street before the second world war, Reidy's the blacksmiths had a house and they leased out the back room to the Union Members. The Transport and General Workers Union were open every Sunday to collect the Union Dues.

CURES FOR A FEW AILMENTS

Old people believed that a very good cure for rheumatism was to get a dead man's skull from the graveyard and grind a piece of it into powder. Having it mixed with milk and brought to the boil. This mixture has to be taken hot. Still on rheumatism a mixture of red pepper and first shot whiskey or poteen rubbed vigorously to the affected parts.

If a person is suffering from yellow jaundice, get someone to hold a lizard down the throat only for a minute.

Burns…Melt some fat of the sheep and get some droppings of a goat, put in a cloth and squeeze the liquid into the melted fat, stir together and spread the like plaster over the burn area you will get instant relief.

Warts. Get a snail, rub the slime over the warts and then take the snail to a Whitethorn bush and impale the snail on one of the thorns.

LAFFORDS FORGE BALLYLOOBY

On entering the village of Ballylooby from the Cahir side, are the ruins of a dwelling and forge, the townland is called Deravoher [oak road].

The land was first purchased on the 19th July 1894 by Billy Lafford From R.H. Henry Ansow, Barron, Waterpark. A vendor of land. The cost of this venture in 1894 was 20 pounds and the amount payable for 49 years was 16 shillings per year. [there is 20 shillings in a pound] Payable on the first day of May and on the first day of November. The total area of the site is less than a quarter acre. Billy Lafford died 1905 and passed the business over to his son Michael Lafford. Michael joined the British Forces for the 1914-1918 war as a Farrier, he and Paddy Egan's father were in Mons and Flanders and both returned alive. Michael returned after the war to operate the forge once again. The last inhabited owner that worked the forge was William [Willie] Lafford, he was small in stature but broad at the shoulder and was known as, The Wren..

The Wren enters another story in a while.

The forge reopened briefly from 1946-1952 after being closed for 7 years. The new tenants were Gerry Deasy and Davy Burke, a carpenter from Whitechurch. They made Horse carts, timber spoked wheels and Banded Cartwheels at the forge. The banding stone, quite a large and very weighty stone, remains on the site.

Blacksmithing is thirsty work and the Wren would take an odd pint like most people. At that time you had to be out of the pub by 9 o'clock except you were living more than 3 miles away. Willie was in Nora Casey's pub only a hundred yards away. The police raided the pub and caught Willie. A summons to appear in court was served on Willie by Detective Gilbert Potter, the man that Dan Breen and others kidnapped and shot dead.

In April 1921 the British held an Irish Republican Thomas Trainor and were to hang him. The republican army kidnapped Potter and used him as a bargaining tool to get Thomas Trainor released. The British did execute the Republican and as a reprisal The Irish Republican Army killed the District Inspector Potter. The Black and Tans then went on a rampage.

TINCURRY

As a reprisal for the Potter killing the Black and Tans, the scourge of all that was decent, went on a trail of destruction and on the night that they bombed Tincurry they destroyed and burned 11 houses of innocent families. Before the degenerates actually blew the house, they took all the furniture out and with sledge hammers and pickaxes reduced it to firewood. They forced the occupants to make them tea as they destroyed their lives.

Tincurry House was built in 1750 on the site of an older house built by a Quaker man called Andrew Jackson, it is across the road from Millgrove House both were Jackson built.

It is a testament to the builder that the Tans were only able to blow half of the house. This happened in 1921, rebuilding began in 1926. Tobins of Tincurry was what we call a safe house; the Irish Republican Army were welcome there when on the run. Marion Tobin was born Mary Ann Carew in Knockgraffon and became Tobin when she married James. They had 3 children May, Eva, John,..She became a widow in 1918. She was a true republican carrying messages in secret and cleaning guns as well as leaving the rebels the use of her land for drilling. She was a staunch member of Cumann Na Mban and holds the distinction of becoming the first Woman Councillor in the country in 1920-1925.

On one night alone Sean Treacy, Dan Breen and Sean Hogan appeared at the door after walking across the Galtees, the big three were the most wanted in the country. There is another safe house still standing only about a mile from Tincurry. It is a climb up to Quarryhole and one of the best locations in the country as a secret hideout.

Following the destruction of her house Marian and the children were taken in at Millgrove House by the Butlers, their neighbours.

On a personal note my grandmother was sent from Scotland as a small child and reared in the poorhouse in Cashel. When she reached 16 years she was sent into service as a maid to Tincurry House in about 1912. My grandfather and Ellen Dodd was her name were married in the poorhouse in Clogheen in 1918, they lived somewhere in Garryroan, I do not know where. Ellen Lonergan died from blood poisoning after standing on a nail in 1945.

DRUNK DRIVING CHARGE AT CAHIR

A Cahir lorry driver, who was stated to have taken off his coat and taken out his false teeth and challenged a Guard to a fight, was, at Clonmel Court, found guilty of driving while drunk. He was Michael Dempsey, Tipperary Road, Cahir, who was charged with the offence and fined 5 pounds. A further charge of dangerous driving on the same occasion at Ballyneety, Ardfinnan, on June 6 was dismissed.

The defendant was ordered to pay £5-18s-6d expenses and had his driver's licence suspended for one year. Recognisances were fixed in the event of an appeal and Justice Skinner said he would allow the licence to be used pending an appeal.

Guard P. Moinseall. Ardfinnan, said that around midnight on June 6th he saw a lorry coming from the Newcastle direction downhill into Ardfinnan. The lorry was weaving from side to side. He decided to stop the lorry and stood under a light to wave it down.

He opened the door and asked the driver his name. The man replied Murphy'..The Guard asked the driver to get out of the lorry and the driver asked the Guard if he would like to drive the lorry. He then got out and stood with his back to the cab door. He started to smoke and when asked to walk a few paces said..that he could not as his feet were sore. He then started to jump up and down on the road.

On the way to the Barracks the defendant started to talk and repeated several times..Buttons and Bows, any chance of a large bottle Guard ? They are all going into space and on the way he did a bit of a step dance. At the Barracks, Guard Rowland and the defendant had a few words and Mr.Dempsey became aggressive and said that he never hit a Guard with his cap on. Guard Rowland removed his cap and the defendant took off his coat and took out his false teeth. He refused to sign the book at the Barracks.

A court case ensued and Dr.Burke, Ardfinnan, was called as a witness the Doctor said that the defendant refused to be examined by him. The doctor noticed that Mr.Dempsey was unsteady on his feet and smelled of

Drink. Justice Skinner asked if these symptoms could be caused by fatigue, The Doctor replied that fatigue does not smell of stout.

Giving evidence Mr .Dempsey said that he left Cahir at 6.45 with his last load of gravel for Ballinamult, he delivered the load and on the way back he came by way of Ballymacarbry and stopped there for a drink.

He met a man that stood him two large bottles and he had two himself. He left for home and going through Newcastle he pulled at Nugent's pub and had a few pints there, he bought a quart of cider for the morning because he worked in a quarry and it was thirsty work. When asked as to why he refused to let the Doctor examine him, he replied that he was afraid of needles because he had been in the army. Matthew Keating, his employer, said that Mr.Dempsey worked for him for 8 years and found that he can be very excitable when among strangers.

Mick Dempsey was a Wexford man that came with the 13 th battalion and lived in Sraid Na Gcuic before moving to Woodview. He was a mechanic by trade ...This cutting was from the Nationalist Saturday July 1st 1961.

SNORNAGOOK—SRAID NA GCUIC

One of the residents that lived in the above street was Pearse Fitzgerald, another character, he was the proud owner of a piebald donkey and foal. At this time in the 60s these piebalds were worth a bit of money, normally you couldn't give away donkeys. He kept the animals in the field behind his house [Woodview had not been built yet]. He used to check on his brood about four times a day, because they were in great demand. He went for a pint to Coltons pub and while he was gone Mick Dempsey brought the foal into his kitchen. Pearse returned and searched for the foal and in a panic ran across town to report the theft to the Guards. Pearse was not a young man and almost got a heart attack with excitement and the run across town. Being in such a state the new squad car brought him back home and of course Dempsey had returned the foal to its mother. Stern words from the Guards for wasting their time.

Mick Dempsey used to have a wireless and a speaker out on the road and the crowd gathered to listen to matches, this was before Television.

MILITARY ATHLETICS

Military athletic events started to become more common from the 1860s. In 1861 at Cahir the non commissioned officers and men,commemorated the anniversary of the Battle of Balaclava with a series of athletic sports in the barrack square. One of the more moving features of the day was the appearance of a horse, Known to the regiment as the ; Donkey , which was ridden in the Charge of the Light Brigade, the famous Crimean disaster.

Events such as running, jumping and feats of skill typically involved members of the military. Where the sports were deemed open, some of the more prominent athletes from all over Tipperary were allowed to participate. Sporting challenges were a common feature of military life.

In October 1882 the prize money on offer at the Cahir military sports ranged from 5s to £1 for 1st place and 2s for second.

The contemporary press reports suggest that the Cahir military were the most innovative when it came to organising a varied programme of events.

DANCING AT THE CROSSROADS

There was a stage at the crossroads at Ballymacadam. Paddy and Josie Mullaney and Tom Corbett used to play the music. Paddy played the bagpipes, it's anyone's guess as to how you dance to bagpipe music. In the good weather the crowds were enormous with no radio or T.V. only talking or dancing. In the event of bad weather Tom Corbett had his own stage at his house and at weekends he held the dances inside his house

Paddy and Josie sold their small holding to the Butcher Kennedy; this was probably Jimmy Kennedy also called Noisey.

INSULT

Two neighbours met Jimmy who was all dressed up in his Sunday best, what's the occasion? asks Tommy, I am retiring from the Council after 40 years. Tommy says; that is a long time to have been doing nothing.

WOODENSTOWN CASTLE

Woodenstown Castle about two miles outside the village of New Inn. A story handed down in the neighbourhood says it belonged to a Carey or Carew, who was in possession of the Castle during one period of its existence.

The same Landlord was as many of this kind a Non Catholic. He may be what the locals call a turn coat he was to put it mildly not of good cheer but full of good red wine.

People say too that not only was Carey a hard man but a cruel one. They say that he actually put the poor tenants to death for non-payment of rent. Often he scourged the workers in charge of his horses and stables and treated his servants no better than dogs.

In a drunken rage of frenzy Carey is said to have gone one day and actually fired shots on the Catholic Church then in Lough Kent graveyard. Disease soon laid him low. His body became so corrupt and loathsome that no one would bear to go near him. He had no funeral and his servants buried his remains under the Castle wall.

ANYONE FOR TENNIS

Born in Marlhill, New Inn on 21st June and died 21st June 1907. Helena Bertha Grace Rice was a member of Cahir Lawn Tennis Club,

and holds the record of being the only Irish woman or man to win Wimbledon Lawn Tennis Championship. In winning the 1890 Wimbledon final she is credited with inventing the ; Overhead Smash ; Helena never married and passed away at the age of 41 in the year 1907

THE DRAPER

Dick Hickey was a well known character that ran a Draper Shop with his wife in Church Street. A customer came in one day looking for a shroud for her deceased husband. How much she asked, 30 shillings, says Dick. I can get it cheaper at Bob Keatings…Get it says Dick and I bet his arse will be out through it in a week.

150 YEARS AGO

Long ago there were about thirty houses built on the mountainside from Ballydrehid to Cahir. These houses were very small, and some of their ruins are still to be seen. The little gardens or ; haggards ; as they were called and the ridges in which they set the potatoes are still to be seen. Some of the houses were covered with thatch, whilst others were covered with heath and sticks. The bed or settle was always in the kitchen and was folded up during the day.

The floors were of clay and there was only one window in each house. A half door was a regular thing to see and yet half-doors are still to be seen in some houses. Turf was always used for the fire and was from the top of the Galtees. Part of the road which led to it is still to be seen. Rushlights were used in the nighttime for light. The rushes were steeped in some kind of fat and they gave out as much light as a candle. Very few of the people had a cow for milk, most of the householders relied on a nanny goat. Cabbage and onions with the potatoes were grown in every garden. All the women wore shawls that they knitted themselves and the men wore jumpers and knitted waistcoats. Chickens and hens wandered during the day but were locked up at night from the fox. At night the inhabitants would gather in each other's houses for storytelling or mending boots during poetry or singing.

Children were taught to read and write their native tongue behind hedges by learned men. There were a few donkeys and drays that everyone shared. The turf was brought down in creels and on the people's backs.

PENAL LAWS

Long ago Mass used to be said under a Whitehorn Bush on an old bohreen in the townland of Toureen. The bush was flat on top and there were flat stones at the base. An alder bush is now growing beside it. Mr.Edward Lonergan lives beside it and he would not cut it down for fear something bad would happen to him. This piece was written before 1900, the Lonergans are still there.

PETTICOAT LOOSE

There are several versions of this tale; this is the one that I grew up with.

Mary Hannigan had a small farm on the Vee road above Clogheen, she and her husband worked the land and had a maid to help out. Mary was a keen dancer and would go to dances every night, if there was one on. At those times dances were held in each other's houses. Mary's husband had not got the passion for jigs and reels as Mary had. On this night one November it was in O'Brien's house that the Celigh was taking place.

Mary dressed in her loose colourful attire and hit off on her own, the music was in full swing and in no time she was on the floor stepping it out. Swinging around in a lively dance, Mary caught her dress on a nail that was protruding from the wall and it pulled the cloth off her, leaving her naked from the waist down. The other dancers thought this bit of misfortune was the funniest thing and they laughed and laughed. Mary ran from the house full of embarrassment and mentally affected. She would never get over this.

Arriving home before she normally would, she entered the house and saw light under her bedroom door, she put her ear to the door and heard her maid's voice and her husbands. This was the last straw in a frenzy she went and got an axe. The crazed woman killed both lovers in her bed.

The Judge passed down a sentence of death by hanging, Mary never recovered her composure and went to her death full of hate and malice.

Mary Hannigan was hanged…... .but this was not the end of her. O Briens house again and late into the night as the dancers were leaving, they saw an apparition. A pale almost white figure with a finger pointing at them saying …I want revenge…. The terrified couples ran for their lives. This spectre of Mary Hannigan appeared every night that the dance was held at O Briens.

The Priest was called and the holy father asked the apparition what she wanted and the ghost of Mary said Revenge The priest condemned the spectre to empty Bay Lough with a thimble until she repents…Mary never did. Never go to the Bay Lough at night.

THE CARD

Willie my neighbour reached 65 and got the pension, he was issued with a card that had several entitlements attached to it.

Willie and his good wife Elizabeth were in the habit of going for a Sunday drive, and the world was their oyster. They could end up anywhere. The couple would have dinner out and take in whatever sights there were.

The loving couple were taking in a national monument that entitled pensioners to a reduction. The bould Willie put his hand in his pocket and announced that he forgot to bring his card. I have nothing to show them he said, his loving wife Liz said ..Just show them your face.

THE BLUE SHIRT

The Blueshirt movement was a fascist grouping that evolved into Fine Gael. Hitler had his Brownshirts, other fascist groups around Europe had their different hues of shirts, Redshirts and so on.

Pakie Cronin was one of a family that moved to England in the early 60s. Pakies father Battie was the town bill poster until he left for Blighty.

There were sites around the town for advertising posters and everyone from Circuses to Dramatic Societies used them. Pakie was in town wearing the Blue Shirt when a Fianna Fail activist shouted across the road for Pakie to take off that shirt. Pakie shouted back…I can't, it is the only one that I have.

ABBEY STREET

Beside the pub that is now called 22 Abbey St. It used to be Coltons at this time. There was an arched double door and upstairs was the Boxing Club. The club was run by a Mr. Hunter and Captain

Beary. Two of the better boxers to fight for the club at the time were Patsy Ward and David Fleming. Tournaments were held in the Parochial hall and the club catered for all ages. At ground level there was a coal merchant called the Bill O. Bill O Connor from New Inn, used to smoke a pipe and sat on a bag of coal playing the Banjo. The Bill O would have known Harry Gleeson and wrote his own book on the events.

EDDIE DALTON

From New Inn, Harry Gleeson was hanged on 23 April 1941 for the killing of Moll Carthy. He was unsuccessfully defended by Sean Mc Bride. The Bill O' Connor wrote a book called the Farcical Trial of Harry Gleeson and how right he was. Eddy Dalton of Golden made it his mission in life to have Harry exonerated. Eddie spent a lot of years unearthing vital evidence to clear Harry's name.

The 6 th April 2015 was the culmination of so many frustrating years when President Michael D Higgins signed a posthumous pardon for Harry Gleeson. Much to the delight of the group and Eddie Dalton. In July 2024 Harry's remains were reinterred at Holy Cross, bringing an end of a saga. It took 80 years to bring him home.

CANVASSING WITH THE MAN

In the general election of 2002 we were in Ardfinnan canvassing for Dennis Landy, Labour Party Candidate for South Tipperary, We had a few heavy hitters with us, Breda Moynahan Cronin, Ruari Quinn and Michael D Higgins the future President. Michael was in great demand and was getting held up at every door. We were in Castle view and planning who went where. Michael D. went to the nearest house and we spread out. The group had finished and there was no sign of Michael. The house that he was in had a Doberman dog but he looked quiet.

After a while Michael appeared, clearly not himself as we walked towards the car he asked me if I knew that woman, I said yes everyone knows Mary. Well he said…I would rather bite the nose off that dog than speak to that woman again.

THE MAN FROM KILCOMMON

Paddy Saunders was in the pub one night arguing with the whole bar, I listened for a while and as I was driving him home in the car I said …you were as wrong as could be…..I know that, he said but I wasn't going to give in. My Mother Bridie Lonergan was at Paddy and Kitty's wedding and she told me that they both fainted at the same time, at the altar.

BALLYBRADO

I think that this translates to the home of the salmon. This House was built in 1879 and designed by Robert Watt the famous arts and crafts influenced architect. When this house was finished the people from all over Ireland came to have a look. They used to say that it was the house that Rashers and Sausages built. The House had 10 live in maids and 10 gardiners as you can imagine the grounds were pristine and still are. On approaching the first thing that catches the eye is the ornate chimneys, all 27 of them. The house and farm now has 230 acres and all in a magical setting with the Suir river running close by. Henry Denny was the owner and he made his money by perfecting new bacon curing techniques. The Denny family would by today's standards be Billionaires. In their Waterford plant they were killing 3,000 pigs a week, in those days that was an enormous amount.

The Denny family remained until 1937 and the family graves are in Kilcommon Graveyard.

The next owners were the Harold-Barrys in 1940, they downsized the main house by pulling a substantial amount of the structure down. The remaining house is now 9.000 sq ft. The Harold-Barrys then opened a Salmon Fishing Hotel; they remained in the house until 1946.

The next to purchase was the Craig-Whites, who were South African and were of the Black and White Whiskey dynasty. That is the whiskey label with the Black and White scottie dogs. The whiskey people remained for 37 years before returning to South Africa.

1983 saw the arrival of Josef and Marianne Finke. Mr Finke said that he went all around Ireland with a view to purchasing a new home, he looked at about 15 premises or estates and when he saw Ballybrado he said ..This is it..

Josef returned to Germany and made preparations for the long journey by tractor from Badkreuznach, Rhineland, near Frankfurt.

This was going to be a once in a lifetime journey. A convoy of tractors and trailers with machinery for milling and accommodation for 5 adults and 5 children, cooking and dining arrangements had to be taken care of. As they loaded the convoy onto the boats for home in Fishguard, the department of Agriculture halted half of the convoy and said that the agricultural machinery had to be disinfected and would not allow the remaining half of the convoy to board and placed it in quarantine for 3 months. Three months later they were organised and ready to start a new life. The original journey took over 4 days and 650 kms by road. The plan was to Pioneer Organic farming, In 1983, this was practically unheard of but perseverance won out. One venture was to bake bread with organically grown flour. This was a great success. They brought their own TVs with them, but the German sets would not work in Ireland. Josef said that they gave 20 years without television and it did no harm.

THE NEW INN BLACKSMITH

Another story told to me by Con Clifford from New Inn, was about a tyrannical Lord that had a castle outside the Village. There was a blacksmith at Lough Kent that was a little hard of hearing. One day in 1850 he was shoeing a horse when the Lord rode up beside him and hit the blacksmith with his whip while shouting at him.

The farrier was startled and by reflex threw the hammer at his Lordship and met him in between the eyes, killing him instantly. It would be little use looking for mercy from the British for killing one of their own. He was packed off to America that day and was never heard from again.

THE HOMESTEAD

John Neville came from Wexford and Nora Hanley came from Kilcommon, Tipperary. They were both employed in Cahir House Garages, John as a Ford Parts storeman and Nora as bookkeeper they married and settled on the Cork rd. The couple built a Bungalow there and were the first people in Cahir to get a Co.Council loan. An avid gardener John won a gold medal and was Ist in Ireland for his Roses. They had a unique idea at the time and built a restaurant on the edge of town. All the other eateries were in pubs. They also had a Filling Station and the venture lasted until the early 90s. when they both retired. Local man Patsy Burke was the builder of the Homestead; it is now a private house. Young John is a guitar and musical instrument maker on site.

WHO'S THE BEST BOY

Paddy Egan of Garryclogher, had a cat called William that was 16 years old. The cat had no teeth and paddy used to feed him with his finger with soft food. The cat loved his owner and the love was returned. About a half kilometre over the road is a wooded area called the Cover. Paddy used to cut firewood there and bring it back to the house in a wheelbarrow. The cat used to wait on a gate pier for his owner and as Paddy passed, the cat would climb on his shoulder and get a lift home, while Paddy praised the animal for his cleverness. This had been going on all summer. One day the cat's owner had something else to do after his lunch, so he cycled to the cover to cut sticks and collect them the following day. When he was cycling home, the 80 year old man on his 80 year old bike was passing the gate pier and William was ready for his lift. He jumped on moving Paddy's shoulder and to gain a hold, had to sink his claws into Paddy's face. As you can imagine this distracted the old man's momentum and he hit the newly paved road head first.

His wife Ellen was at the kitchen sink, when the door crashed open and her blood covered husband was screaming. I'll kill the bastard, where's the poker.?. Ellen thought that he had been hit by a car and wanted to do the driver some damage, what happened she asked, trying to clean some of the blood from his deeply scratched face, that bastard of a William almost killed me....The cat had the sense to give Paddy a wide berth for a week or two. He recovered and peace was made, Paddy wore his wounds with pride.

SUIRVALE HOUSE

At the junction of the Old Cashel road and Priests road is the historical pile called Suirvale house, once called Abbey View. The house was once owned by a Major General Harris who met a sad end in the house.

The General was an Irishman in the British Army and should be remembered as the person that was responsible for disbanding the dreaded, B. Specials in the north of Ireland. The B.Specials were a Black and Tan version of a police force brought in by the British to intimidate the Catholic population in Northern Ireland.

CHICAGO

Myra and Pat Carroll were from Carlow and went to America to work and make their fortune. Whatever about making their fortune they made 5 children and decided to return to Ireland. The couple bought a farm of land in Roosca Burke..

The children grew and some returned to the States for different amounts of time. Pat passed away and Myra was left to carry the can. She was a very capable woman, who could turn her talent to almost anything except driving..You would always know that Myra was on the way with gears grinding, she was used to automatic cars.

Myra's maiden name was Standish and would be of the Leap Castle Standish,,,,the most haunted Castle in the country. Part of the Castle is still occupied today.

Pat junior has a house in Florida and his next door neighbour is Brendan Carroll the Dublin comedian, no relation.

GRUBB'S GRAVE

There was a miller named Mr. Grubb, who lived during the famine, he came from Castlegrace. He died and was brought to an usual burial place. Told to me by Mr Grubb's relative.

His request was to be buried high up on the Knockmealdown Mountains, above the Vee. Along with his dog and gun, because he wanted to oversee his house and lands, where he spent a most joyous existence. He was a great family man and a good father. His request was granted and he was taken to his last resting place not without incident. A relative of his told me that he left orders that the men that would be bearing his remains, were to be looked after with refreshments. The mistake that was made was opening the whiskey and stout before the body was eventually at its last resting place.

He was brought by road on a horse and dray and then the climb up the steep mountain, was by a group of well oiled pallbearers. Of course it took twice as long as estimated because the deceased was dropped several times before reaching the designated spot.

THE DUTCH CONNECTION

In the winter of 1690. Godert De. Ginkel Ist Earl of Athlone a Dutchman, given the title by William of Orange. He was coming from the siege of Limerick on his way back to the Netherlands. He needed a suitable site to rest his army and chose the spot by the river to rest his army in safety he selected Tankerstown.Christmas 1690 Hugh Massey visited Ginkel on a mission of some urgency; it seems that the local Irish insurgents were threatening to burn him out. He obtained 40 Dragoons to protect his house. He made haste on his return to Dentrileague only to find his mansion house on fire. Unable to put out the flames he had to bed down in the stables. I remember in the 1980s Seamus Dalton telling me that one day, when he was ploughing that field where the army camped, he hit the plough off something heavy. He thought it was a rock at first, but it turned out to be a small cannon, left behind by Ginkel's army. It is now in the Dublin Museum. Stemming from when the army was camped for the winter, it is said that Dutch blood abounds in Kilmoyler.

SAMUEL BURKE

Samuel Burke had some very lucrative businesses in and around Cahir. Hardware, Glass warehouse Milling and stores. In the 1930s Samuel knew how to live it up. When he wanted to go fishing he would catch the train to Tipperary but he would halt the train at Ballydrehid outside Mr Peters house and go for breakfast with him and both would hit off fishing until dinner and then he would stop the mail train to bring him home again. By all accounts he was a good employer and a very popular man. Sam lived in Kilemny. Samuel had a brother Richard, who was a little work shy and liked Horse Racing and the odd punt. He was Master of the Foxhounds. He liked a game of cards and was an excellent dancer. Our boy never missed a hunt ball no matter where it took place. Richard went to the United States it can be said not by choice. As luck would have it he hit San Francisco and met and married a lovely woman, an American Millionairess, he never bothered with Cahir again.

NICKNAMES

Out the Khyber road long ago there was Slaughter Guts Duggan.

An old Traveller woman in Cahir.   Lizzie the Fluther.

Another woman long ago.   Jude the Two.

A scrap man in Ballyhicky.   Mick the Mowler

Bunty Burke, Snornagook.   Sawdust.

Cathrine Walsh.   Kitty the Hare.

!st World War veteran.   The Blue Donnell.

Frank Hogan.   The Horse.

Paddy Saunders.   Hank.

Vince Lonergan.   Rinso.

Tom Beary.   Captain

Liam O Brien.   The Honk.

Willie Irwin.   Chicken.

John Murphy.   Spud.

Dennis Murphy.   The Dinger.

Tom Donoghue.   Dingle.

Martin Cashman.   Murty.

LITTLE BITS

The late 1990s a very old widow woman from Cappauniack, discovered the Cahir day Care Centre and it made a huge difference to her life. Stacia Nagle, a shortened version of Anastacia, played the melodeon and entertained all. Herself and Frank Hogan who played the harmonica were a double act at the Centre and I hope someone recorded the duo.

In the 50s and 60s nearly every one with a house would keep a lodger. Commercial Travellers had a regular round weekly and had some place in every town. These men were a popular catch, because in those days work was scarce and money was scarcer, and a commercial traveller was considered a good job.

A Man called Innocent Callaghan from Kilmoyler had his head chopped off at Boytonrath for his part in the 1898 rebellion.

In the 1890s the hurlers took the game seriously, at a local match in Dranganmore a man called Kearney was killed on the field of play when a row broke out over a decision.

The Whitehead Byron from Kilmoyler, a Fenian, who was Colonel in the Union Army in America returned to fight for Ireland. Was arrested and deported to Van Diemans land for life.

On The way into St Pecauns beside the railway is a tall tree and it is a Crimean Elm. That is pretty rare.

The remains of the old Church on Old Church St was last used for worship in the 1820s. As can be identified by the double bell tower, it was used by the Protestant and Catholic worshippers. A different sounding bell for each. There was a curtain wall inside to keep them apart and outside the Catholics were buried on one side and the others opposite. This was considered a giant leap forward for both sects. It did not seem to work as they both went and built their own Churches.

THE CAHIR FIRE BRIGADE

This story was doing the rounds in the 1980s. Maybe there is some truth in it.

There was a cat up a tree in the mall and a woman who had absolutely nothing else to do reported this to the Guards. She demanded immediate action. The Guard on duty told the woman that the cat would come down when it's ready, he said that they always do. She wasn't having any of it call the fire brigade she demanded. The Volunteer Firemen arrived and as usual a crowd gathered and everyone knew each other. The ladder was put against the tree and a fireman ran up the ladder but the cat ran up higher, out of reach of the fireman. A conference was held by the volunteers because the ladder was the longest they had. They looked a picture in their fireman's hats and oilskins when a suggestion was made to wet the cat with the hose and he would come straight down. It is difficult to dampen a cat with a high pressure hose .The man on the hose aimed straight at the unfortunate animal and blew him off the tree into the river. Panic stations..someone grabbed a life buoy and threw it into the water in an attempt to save the cat. The life buoy struck the cat and it went under, never to be seen again. The nosey woman blamed the Volunteers and the Firemen said that she should in future mind her own business. The crowd sided with the Fire Brigade.

CLUBS

There were several clubs in town, up to the 1970s, one was the Legion Club down St.Marys road. The Cahir House Hotel has taken over the building where it was. Working men used to go to play cards and snooker and billiards or just have a chat. Remember this was before Television so life was totally different. The Jubilee Nurses house, again taken over by the hotel, was a reading room, a club where people went to read newspapers and the like. There was another reading room next to the Roma restaurant. These were reading and smoking and were mostly for men. These reading rooms were closer to the1900s.

THE FIRE ON THE SQUARE

The shop was Baff Carew's sweet and general grocer shop and it stood where O'Briens chemist is now. The building was completely razed to the ground. Every house at that time had a storage place for coal inside the house, mostly under the stairs called the coal hole. One of the reasons for the blaze was that there was hot coal found its way into the coal hole.

The date was 18th August 1937, when the fire started under the stairs. The locals for years referred to it as the fire in the square. Jerry Sheehan witnessed the burning as did Paddy Walsh who was getting a lift on Mara's horse and float. Mara's were delivering all kinds of supplies to the shops in town, from the Railway Station.

Jerry Sheehan told me that he won £100 from Fintan Moore over the date of the blaze.

A BOB'S A BOB WITH BOB

Castle St. Bob Keating owned a draper shop that was unique in Cahir.

Bob himself was unique as he had this fixation of washing the footpath by throwing buckets of water almost all the time. There was an electricity pole outside his premises and Bob had clothes and wellingtons hanging way up the pole as well as an awning, he had more blankets and shawls and every thing that was in the shop hanging from. It was impossible to walk the footpath. It is well known that the Rolling Stones were passing and stopped to have a look. Bob ran them off with a bucket of water. 15. Feb. 1971 saw the advent of decimalisation for all the country except Bob, he refused to display his prices in the new Euro, but kept to Pounds Shillings and Pence for the rest of his days.

The Headline on the Sunday Mirror..A bobs a bob with Bob.

THE POUND

Where the Garda Barracks is now this field used to be the town pound. For anyone that doesn't understand, the pound meant impound. The place where stray animals were impounded until their owners turned up to claim them. This piece of land in Cahir the owners were known as Lonergans the pound. Years ago cattle and horses were always straying on the road.

BOYCOTTING IN CAHIR.

Patrick O Donnell reported to Land league Offices in Dublin on the funeral in Cahir which nobody attended. On December 31st 1880, The Shrewsbury Chronicle; covered the event under the headline

Boycotting a corpse; The article outlines the circumstances in which a Cahir farmer paid his rent, when his mother died...Certain parties desired to show their disapproval and boycotted the funeral. Only one mourner attended the funeral.

In 1885 Cahir Publican David O Gorman's licence was up for renewal.

The Constabulary objected because O' Gorman had engaged in boycotting by refusing to sell liquor to emergency men. David O Gorman does not appear to have regained his licence. In 1891 his grocery and premises on the Square were up for sale.

The Cahir correspondent noted that boycotting was proceeding at an alarming extent. He gave the example of a person who had lent an agricultural implement to another, who took a farm from which a tenant was evicted for non-payment of rent. The man received a threatening letter warning him not to provide any further assistance to the alleged offender. He gives another example of a farmer near Cahir who had also taken over a farm of an evicted tenant. The man's horse was maliciously killed and a valuable dog destroyed, together with other malicious acts. The correspondent reported the Police were unable to trace the perpetrators being afforded no information by the Cahir people.

In 1890 E.Mc Cuaig, a grocer in Cahir was boycotted for assisting the Smith-Barry's and Going and Smith flour millers, Cahir, and in Mitchelstown the Society of Co Operative Bakers refused to work with their flour. They had been selling their flour to the agents of the Smith=Barry estate. The firm was forced to formally apologise for their actions to the Cahir branch of the Irish National League.

In 1881, The boycotted landlord Mr. Bright was unable to obtain a room at any Inn in Cahir to collect his rent.

DAVID FITZGERALD

He is buried beneath a Celtic Cross in Kilaldriffe Cemetery, not far from his birthplace in Ballydrehid Cahir.

He was born in1897 and died in 1933 from cancer, To access his home place you would have to cross the railway tracks at the Khyber, he was the son of Michael and Bridget and his mother said he had more brains than anyone that she knew. He had a more interesting short life than most men. He was a republican socialist, who with Peadar O Donnell instigated the Peasants and Farmers party as well as Saor Eire. He was imprisoned for revolutionary work. He was imprisoned in Mountjoy and escaped. He travelled to Moscow and lived there for a while. This action ensured that he was always under the British eyes. All the information that you need is on line.

PRESIDENT OF THE IFA

Joe Rea was President of the IFA for 4 years and it seemed like forever. Joe was going home on a very bad night of rain and wind. About a half mile from his destination in the lashing rain, on the road in front of him was a man lying on the ground in pouring rain. Rob McGrath was building a house right beside where the body was lying. Joe jumps out of his Mercedes and leaves the comfort of the car to help the man.

He shook the man and shouted Rob ..Rob wake up, he felt for a pulse there was one. In frustration he grabbed the collars of his coat and dragged the man across the muddy front lawn into the nearest room. He put the drunken man into the bed without removing his clothes. All this was done in the pitch dark. Joe rubbed his chest as his heart was not too good. Soaked and breathless and covered with mud he made his way back to his car. Sitting in his car, the lights of another car approached and pulled up. Sean Irwin, a pub owner was bringing home his customers, and out of the car got Rob McGrath and said goodnight Joe.......This a true story the man on the road was a Mr.Dunne.

BARREL TOP

The early 2000s down our way the last of the Traveller barrel top wagons that used to travel on the old roads. They avoided the busy roads and motorways. The Rileys came around our way every few months. They had names like Step and a Half, Curly and Fortycoats, there were always 5 of them, some slept in the Barrel top and they used to make a tent from sally branches and a sheet of canvas. They had a donkey to pull the wagon. Garryroan was one of their halting stops, then they would move over the road to the Rath before parking up at Garryclogher schoolhouse. The last time that the Rileys came around their wagon went up in flames. There was not enough time to call the Fire Brigade because the fire was so intense that it disappeared in minutes. When the smoke cleared all that was left was the axle, the little cast iron stove and about a stone of nails. The roof was canvas painted with tar to waterproof it. The scene of the five people standing there beside the spot where their home had been, will stay with me forever. Paddy Egan arrived with a gallon of tea and biscuits as an attempt to give solace.

Another Traveller man used to come around and always camp at the Rath, he could be called a Tinker because he knew the trade. Dan Veale could make almost anything that he put his mind to, Dan could make a copper kettle on the side of the road that would not leak. His tools were a hammer, tinsnips and nine inches of railway track as an anvil.

In the old days Dan would be in town mending buckets and washing basins as well as putting edges on knives and scissors. Dan used to live in a modern caravan, but the one thing missing was a car. I was asked several times to tow him to the next town.

Mary Carthy was an old woman when I knew her in my teens. She was centred in Ardfinnan but used to walk to Cahir and Ballylooby. She always drank a large bottle of stout, If she felt like sleeping she would just lie on the side of the road and pull the black shawl around her and nod off. She was welcome in Crissy Sheehy's Ballylooby and Archie Condons in Cahir. Mary was very popular with most people, she belonged to an age long gone. She eventually got a house in Ardfinnan.

THE SILVER SANDS

On Friday December 1st 1967 saw the grand opening of ; The Silver Sand Saloon ; at Ballydrehid. The new owner was Matt Keating the sand and gravel man and the management team was Phil Richardson and his lovely wife. Matt Keating purchased the Public house and lands from O Dohertys of Kilmoyler in 1964. The huge lounge was used for ballad sessions and every weekend some big bands. These were the days before the breathalyser and there were lots of these lounges around the country. The Silver Sands Saloon was probably the best known.

The crowds on the opening night were just enormous, cars were parked on the road at each side for hundreds of yards, because the car park was over full. They came to hear the : Wolfe Tones : as the main attraction. The support acts were Noreen and the Raparees…Pat Ryan and his Electrovox and the MC was Paddy Ryan. There was no cover charge.

The Lounge was about 3 miles west of Cahir and it was a popular venue for years, The breathalyser was introduced also called the Bag, that was the death knell for the country pubs. One of the biggest attractions on weekends was a group called Kims People. All the young bucks went to see the Beautiful Blond lead singer.

DERRYNAFLAN CHALICE

The Chalice was part of a larger hoard of altar vessels found by Michael Webb and his son also Michael. The vessels stemmed from the 9th century and were found on a monastic site in ruins a few miles from the Horse and Jockey Hotel, that is also near Killenaule. The pair were using a metal detector after a short time on site. They heard the beep beep and their lives were changed forever.

Sotheby's valued the hoard 6 to 7 Million … .The Irish museum's initial offer was 10 thousand. Needless to say Michael and his son braved it out for a reasonable sum. Michael and his family lived in Clonmore Cahir at the foot of the Galtee Mountains. The Chalice is in the National Museum in our capital City and is often compared to the Ardagh Chalice.

RIAN BO PADRAIG

Rian Bo Padraig : is an early ecclesiastical highway, linking the ancient holy centres of Cashel in Co Tipperary and Lismore in Co Waterford. St. Patricks Road passes down through Mortlestown. When St.Patrick had baptised King Aengus in Cashel, he turned south to go and see his Christian community in Ardmore. The road ran in a straight line, some of which is missing nowadays.How did it get its name ? It seems that Saint Patrick had security travelling with him as well as other clerics, as well as sheep and cows for food. It is said that he was just near Ladys Abbey when the cow gave birth to a calf. They decided to stay in Ballybacon for the night. They blame a Ballybacon man for stealing the calf in the middle of the night. The cow missed her calf so much that she turned around and ran all the way back to Cashel. Hard to believe but it is folklore. This is a very important road and every quarter of a mile along the side of it, there are ringforts, most of which are still there today, only a field or two back from the road.

They put a gate up at Loughkent and when they closed the gate it would be opened when you turned your back. That's the way it is, you can never keep the gate closed. The road came down by Tierneys on the left, past Englishs, through Hallorans yard and on to a gap called Barley Araig, meaning the red earth. It travels down through Mortlestown to the Keylong and on to Ballingeary and Knockfee cross. The name Ballingeary is attached to the wood in John Shines, which is the last remnant of ancient woodland left around here. It means: The Mouth Of The Wood ; in translation.

The road goes down through Molls Cross, there was a woman called Moll living there years ago. It goes on to Loughloher where it staggers up to the Castle and back again, then on another mile to Lough Alice.

Other folklore . The legend relates how Saint Patrick's cow quietly grazing on the bank of the river Tar, had its calf stolen by a cattle thief, from Killwatermoy or somewhere south of the river Bride in County Waterford. The cow sets out in pursuit of the thief and calf. The supernatural beast eventually recovers the calf, Leaving in its wake the deep raked and furrowed route that was forever to be called : Rian Bo Padraig : or the track of Saint Patrick's Cow.: Thanks to Ger O Brien.

KNOCKFEE

Cnoc Fiaidh is Irish and means Stags Hill. Knockfee is a remnant of the Irish Forest which ran all the way back towards Fethard. This forest gave lots of problems to Cromwell on his journey out of Cahir as he travelled to Fethard In the Cromwellian settlements, the Baron of Cahir gave many parts of the old area to his cousins the Butlers Of Ormond. Some of those areas were sublet. Knockfee and Ballylegan were sublet to the Bagwells of Marlfield. The Bagwells put a Protestant into it who built himself a red brick house there. The bricks could still be seen up to 40 years ago..Mr.Ned Kelly told a story of the people of Cahir travelling out to Knockfee during the famine in the hope of getting a turnip or two. The man laid in wait for them to arrive and shot them in the drills.

KEYLONG

Keylong is a very long narrow townland stretching about 3 miles in length. It is very unusual as it is only one field wide all along.

It's said that a landlord was giving a dowry to his daughter. The prospective husband would have to ride a horse as far as he could while swinging a rope with a key tied to it. The man started out on his horse but his arm got tired and the width of the fields got narrower and narrower. He had to settle for what the deal was and was the owner of a very long field. It became the boundary between the Butler Estates and the English planters on the other side. The people on the Butler side were more secure in their tenancy than the other side.

MOLLS CROSS AND KNOCKA

Another incident that happened at Knockagh was when George Plant was visiting IRA men, he travelled up from Dungarvan through Ardfinnan, he met up with a man called Lonergan and they were arrested at Knockagh Cross by the free state army. George Plant is still commemorated every year in St Johns beyond Fethard.

THE BELL AT ROCKWELL

Con Clifford, now long gone, lived in New Inn and told this story but he omitted the names, but swears that it happened in the 1930s.There was a man's body found some way out the Cashel road from New Inn. The guards had a suspect and arrested him but they had no proof. The coroner said that the man was killed at 12 o'clock and the suspect had an alibi. He said that he was in Garranlea at 12, because he asked a gentleman with a pocket watch the time, just as the bell in Rockwell was ringing at noon. A champion runner was brought in to see if he could have been at the murder scene at the time stated, the champion could not do it. The suspect had been charged and was to go to trial in Dublin that winter. The Village of New Inn were all convinced that he would be found guilty. The only witness was a very respectable man and would not move from his testimony. The dead man's family had no doubt in their minds that he would hang. The court lasted only a day and the jury were gone for a short while, as there was a reliable witness. The chairman of the jury announced the verdict of Not guilty,,The chief suspect walked across the city and boarded a ship bound for America. He was never seen again.The deceased man is interred in Boytonrath graveyard. The winter passed into spring and as summer approaches some villages turn their clocks to summer time by putting the clocks forward an hour and others do it at a different day. It was only then that the penny dropped, they never factored in the missing hour.

COLTON'S BAR AND RESTAURANT

Abbey St. there was a pub run by Hughie Colton and his sister Sis. They ran a very successful business, The bar was a favourite with the locals and was full of good characters. Hughie in his earlier days was a chef on board ship. He never was in a hurry to get his customers out early at night. This conversion took place through the front door letterbox. The Guards called after hours and enquired ..is there anyone on the premises ? Hughie answered that there was nobody there, the Guard asked as to why all the lights were on, I would like to see you sweep up this joint in the dark…. Came the reply.

BOOKIES

On the Tipperary Road out of Cahir is the tiny townland called Gurteen. At one time home to a man called Michael Walshe, Michael and his wife who came from Abbey Street had a farm just on the edge of town. As well as having a piece of land Michael was a Bookmaker. For years he was an on-course bookie, and he had two shrewd men who always were with him, Dan Hackett who lived on Old Church St. and Ned O'Halloran that came from Upper Cahir Abbey. Michael had a son Gerard and a daughter Adrienne, who's birthday is 7th June, the day Michael passed away.

One day at the races in Clonmel a punter had a very big win, he came to collect his winnings, leaving the boys with very little cash. Dan asked him what he did for a living,,Ships Captain came the reply. The retort from Dan was ..Pity it wasn't the Titanic.

AWAY WITH THE FAIRIES

Ring forts abound all over the County of Tipperary. They were shelters for families and in some cases tribes. The idea was to have pointed wooden stakes all around the perimeter to keep wild animals and unfriendly neighbours at bay. At that time thousands of years ago there were lots of wild animals like wolves and bears and a lot of big elk. On the mountain road above Cahir, there are a pair of perfect examples, after all these years they have lasted through the ravages of time.

An archaeologist said that we have the fairies to thank for having so many remaining. Only for the fairies and superstition we probably would not have them.

Kyle graveyard is the one near Moorstown Castle. The walls of the Church are completely intact today. The last local person to be buried there was Tom Buckley of Husseystown, who was buried there in 1961.

He was 82. His grandchildren John English and Mary Cormac remember going across the fields in the snow to the funeral. The last caretaker of Kyle graveyard was Jim Hanrahan.

THE ALLEY POND

This was a popular meeting place for men on a summer evening. Folklore says that there was a Ball Alley there but there are no ruins of it visible today. When water was scarce in the summertime, local farmers would drive the animals there for water. Jimmy Hyland from Husseystown remembers the very dry summer of 1959 when there was no rain from June to October, and the pond went dry. Jimmy Hyland from Ballingeary cleaned it out with the bucket on the back of his tractor. This was the most modern digger in the area at the time.

THE BARRETTS OF TINCURRY

In 1825 Andrew Barrett was farming on the mountainside in Tincurry. The present resident John Barrett was told not to drink the water from the mountain as it was overloaded with iron. The Tincurry townland shares a piece of the mountain with another townland called Quarryhole or Poulaculleare, where iron was mined in ancient times. The mines were pockets dug into the mountainside and not mine shafts. John's grandson is the sixth generation to reside in that location and they all have been drinking the water since the 1800s with no ill effects. Andrew lived to be 91 in hard times. The department of health still insists that it is not safe to drink. John's late wife Josephine, used to be a confectioner and I can bear testament to her baking, iron or not. That she baked the best cakes in all of Ireland.

BALLYLOOBY CHURCH

The parish with a farm, every priest that gets appointed to Ballylooby has a farm at his disposal while he remains as Parish Priest. This has nothing to do with the story. Fr.Billy Meehan was at this time residing as PP in the village. One Sunday a man called Murphy and his wife arrived by car, as they usually had a pony and trap. Fr. Billy was watching as the old man got out of the car and went to the passenger side, he was there for ages, Billy went to investigate. The old man was on his knees and could not remove the seat belt from his wife. She is caught in the tackling father, he says.

GALTEE HONEY FARM

Micheal Mac Giolla Coda from Glencar Co.Kerry settled in Cahir on the 31 March 1969 and was A forestry researcher, after travelling all around Ireland he was eventually appointed to Glengarra Forest and remained to this day. His present location is home to over 200 colonies of Native Irish Black Honey bees, a threatened species.The hives are placed all around the near counties. The venture is now run by Michaels daughter Aoife, a Beekeeper now but qualified as a graphic designer.

Michaels father was also a beekeeper so it is in the blood. When he came up from Kerry to his home at Glengarra, he took with him 6 hives from his Kerry home.

Michael is very well known world wide for his work in the scientific end of keeping bees. He bred a bee that was very docile and not as aggressive as the imported kind. He tells us that the Native Irish bee is at risk from these unscrupulous people that bring in foreign bees.

Michael and other like minded people set up the Galtee Bee Keeping group with 4 members. This then evolved into the 32 county Native Honey Bee Society, with over 100 members. They used to have their meetings in the band room, courtesy of Eamon Williams.

Talking to Michael on May day 2024 he tells me that he is 91 and that his father was born in 1870 and his father and uncle fought in the Boer war with the Scots Guards. Michael observes all the local traditions and when there is a death in the family, you must tell the bees, and observe the May Day traditions.

WEATHER FORECASTERS

In the 1930s The Irish Folklore commission wanted every school in the country to get stories from their parents and commit them to paper. The pupils wrote about almost all subjects, here are two about the weather.

When a cat washes her face and puts her paws over her ears the weather is going to be bad.

When a cat sits with her back to the fire while sleeping the weather is going to turn cold.

ST PECAUNS

Toureen on the Tipperary Road is the location of St. Pecauns holy well. This well pattern has been observed for hundreds of years. Every August the locals hold children's sports in the little field in reverence to the Saint. Pecaun came to Toureen in the year 680 following the Synod of Whitby. He was an English monk sent by the Female Church Leader of the Catholic Church. The British and the Vatican Catholics were in disagreement about the Easter arrangements. The Vatican won out in the end. The Holy Well itself is worth seeing as well as the remains of his beehive shaped little shelter. Across the stream is the ruin of a tiny church and many ancient carvings. Of course there is a legend that is attached to the holy place.

There is a stone in a little cage about five inches round, with indentations on it, that are supposed to be made by a woman's fingers.

The legend goes that, Pecaun boiled some potatoes outside his church and he could have a bit of butter to finish the job. A woman passing saw the Saint and she hid the butter behind her back. The holy man asked her for a taste of butter, she denied that she had any. This made Pecaun angry and he turned the butter into the rock that is on site now.

To gain access you have to cross the rail track and go through a little farmyard, Courtesy of a Mr Burke..

IRWIN'S PUBLIC HOUSE

One of the oldest pubs in Cahir. In the 70s it used to be a grocery and hardware store as well as a public bar. In the famine times it was a hospital and the back lounge was the Mortuary. In my younger days it was Willie Irwin that ran the bar and on his death his brother Sean took over. In the hardware part Mary Irwin. Seans aunt .. served behind the counter Miley Flynn and Pat Joe Regan were employed there. In the rear of the pub stands the oldest house in Cahir, the main road used to pass close to the house and exit through the archway. The corners of the house are rounded to allow axles of horse wagons to move freely.

BIANCONI

Born in Italy 24 September 1786 and died Clonmel 1875 and is buried in Boherlahan. Charles Bianconi was the founder of public transport in Ireland. He had mail coaches and coaches that carried 8 and 19 passengers. His first route was from Clonmel, Hearns Hotel to Cahir The Galtee Inn, horses used to be changed at both places after their 2 hour journey. To travel on Bians coach as they were called cost one and a quarter pennies per mile.

The idea came to Charles because of the tax on carriages, the middle class could not afford both. His business grew and grew and in 1865 Charles was earning £35.000 a year, a veritable fortune in those days.

His business lasted for a century, he lived in Clonmel and married an Irish woman Eliza Hayes, they had a family. He was twice Mayor of Clonmel his business was responsible for a lot of Inns around the country, as horses had to be watered and people had to eat.

Before Bianconi some of the populace used to come from Clonmel to Cahir by supply boat and it took 8 hours.

CARRIGEEN CASTLE

Stemming from the 16th century it was an ideal location for a defensive structure, as time passed the structure suffered many changes, In 1813 construction of the present design and shape of the new Bridewell in Cahir. A Bridewell is a small town Gaol and this building had only 5 cells to hold miscreants. The cost of the building at that time was an enormous 2.000 pounds. During the Great Hunger the amount of cells increased to eight cells; interestingly three cells were for women and one room for drunks.. Because there were 8 cells that did not mean that there were only eight prisoners, at times it held over 50, awaiting the Assizes in Clonmel .

David Butler purchased the pile in 1919. His son Sean and his wife Margaret.. Peig…renovated the structure and in 1976 opened the building to guests which was hugely popular and unique. The view from the battlements is just spectacular.

CAHIR ABBEY

The Priory of the Virgin Mary was in 1220 built for the Augustinians by a Norman Knight Galfrid De Camville. The last Prior Edmond Lonergan was made Vicar of the Parish Church of the Virgin Mary of Cahir.

He surrendered the church to Henry VIII the same year. As it was deemed a parish Church it could not be given to the Crown, during the dissolution of the Monasteries. The remaining buildings outside of the Church were given to Sir Thomas Butler Barron of Cahir in 1542. Thomas Married Elenore Butler and they lived in Cahir Castle. Up to the 1990s there were people being buried in the Abbey Graveyard. The last man that I remember was Hugh Coyle, a shoemaker from Abbey Street.

MURDER IN CLOGHEEN

Richard Burke from Cahir, Clerk of Clogheen Workhouse in 1842 aged 47 married Joanna aged 48 and moved to Ennistymon as head of Workhouse, In 1850 moved to Waterford, he got Typhoid but survived. At that time he earned £250 a year. His wife stayed in

Clogheen and he stayed in the Waterford Arms Hotel, seeing his wife only occasionally she gets no money from him. In 1861 there is a scandal, a priest accuses him of rape and three other women accuse him of sexual abuse but these charges are disregarded. The case is reported in the Papers but he is exonerated. His wife Joanna hears and reads the reported accounts and is not happy, his marriage is now on the rocks. 1862 his wife visits him in Waterford, they have an argument and she returns to Clogheen, In March 1862 he tries reconciliation and he writes her a few nice letters. She dies suddenly a short time afterwards, there is suspicion of foul play and her stomach is removed for an inquest. It was claimed that she died poisoned by strychnine. Her husband had said that he would send her medicine, Richard had sent her poison mixed with coffee, witnesses said he procured the poison at the workhouse. A trial ensued. He was found guilty and sent to Clonmel to be hanged. He was hanged by an unknown hangman. Ironically Joanna's cousin died in Australia a few weeks later and left her 7,000 Australian pounds.

THE GREAT ESCAPE

John O'Leary of Knockballineiry, Goatenbridge, told me this story about his father Edward [Ned]. His father was a member of the Old IRA. Ned O'Leary was being held in Clonmel Jail, when he and the rest of the prisoners planned a breakout, the only way out was to dig, but how were they to do it without implements. All they had was the dinner spoons and a few small bits of iron. The engineer in charge was a man called Cooney from Irishtown Clonmel.

Ned was at home hoeing turnips when the free state soldiers came for him. They took the 22 year old to the Borstal that was being used as a holding prison before being taken to the Curragh.

The prison break was the most daring that was seen during the Civil War. The prisoners dug a tunnel 36 yards long, using only kitchen implements. On 28th August 1921, some 36 prisoners crawled through the tunnel to freedom. They exited into an old wood yard, the engineer Cooney had a fall and broke his leg. He was captured Immediately. Some of the prisoners were caught soon after but the most escaped. Ned returned to a safe house that was owned by a man called Pakie Burke, outside Goatenbridge. Some time later the Free State soldiers were coming down the road and Ned's sister saw them, she wanted to warn her brother, she ran to where the safe house was and was seen by the army. They followed her and arrested Ned. While they were bringing him towards Clonmel the truck stopped several times in the hope that Ned would try to escape, then they could shoot him. He was sentenced to 12 years in the Curragh. While he was there he shared a cell with Frank Aiken. Ned was released after serving 9 months, they were given a train ticket home. In Ned's case it was Cahir station and he walked home to Goatenbridge from the station. After the escape there was an enquiry as to how it could happen. They found that discipline was very lax and that security was ignored in most areas. The O'Learys are still farming at the foot of the Knockmealdowns.

The O'Leary homestead is near the Liam Lynch Monument. The monument is a round tower that was erected near the spot where Liam Lynch was shot.

THE TITANIC

There were four people from the Cahir area that were passengers on the ill fated Titanic. They purchased their tickets from Pat Clarke, Castle Street Cahir, who was a travel booking agent for the White Star Line. Roger Tobin age 20 years was from Ballycarron he was lost, Kate Connolly age 35, lost. Katie Peters age 26 lost and Katie McCarthy age 24 saved, she was rescued by the Carpathian, a ship that came to the rescue. The girls were from Ballydrehid and Kilmoyler.

Locals tell me that Roger Tobin and Katie McCarthy were going out together and that Katie McCarthy and Katie Peters were best friends.

THE TOP THIRTY

In The 1980s there was a Cahir rock band that reached the British top thirty. Anything Goes was an RTE production and the boys were guests on that as well, The Band was Media and the line up was Joe Shine, Johnny Casey, Charlie O Neill and Pat Buckley. The discs were Desdemona and Give it an Inch.

FACTION FIGHTING IN ARDFINNAN

Faction Fighting originated in Tipperary in the late 1700s and was carried out mostly in Munster. It involved parishes and villages and even the fighting was between families. A faction fighting stick was the weapon that was used by the men, this was usually a blackthorn about three feet long with a knob at one end, hazel or ash were also used. The women when they took part used a woollen sock with rocks in it. Women could not take part if their husbands were involved. The Church for hundreds of years tried to prevent the fights taking place.

The fair field in Gormanstown on the Clogheen road, was where the horse fair was held. This was the largest for miles around. The British army barracks in the nearby towns were always purchasing horses to keep their numbers up. Two factions that were always having scores to settle were gathering to do battle. Ballybacon and Newcastle factions were mingling among the huge crowds. Word was sent to Cahir barracks that there was trouble brewing, so the powers that be, sent twenty cavalry troopers to discourage any violence. The 8th Hussars arrived looking fierce with their strong animals and lances. What happened next took the Cavalry by surprise. Both factions consisting of several hundred swarthy men wielding sticks, joined forces and ran the British off the field. The priest from Ardfinnan stepped in and told the stickmen that should they continue with the fight, none of them would darken the door of the Church again. The fighters were more afraid of the priest than anyone. The Newcastle men were not happy with this and went home by way of Ballybacon and damaged several houses on their way. There was an old woman living in Gormanstown and leaning on her half door, said… the day is gone and there has not been a blow struck. In an attempt by the Government of the day to bring a halt to the fighting, they banned all the big fairs and markets in Tipperary. Two factions in Kerry around that time had a fight on Ballyea Strand; there were around 1500 on each side and 16 died that day.

REHILL CORNER

Jim Tobin lived in Rehill corner and raised 9 Children there they were all called affectionately the Whiteheads because of being blond. Jim always worked around timber and one of his sons has his own Sawmill. Jim had a cousin that lived in America, the families are still in touch, Maurice Tobin became Mayor of Boston and was Governor of Massachusetts as well as Member of the House of Representatives. The main bridge is named after him The Tobin Bridge in the city of Boston. Back in the 1930s Maurice sent a wind charger to Jim at Rehill and the Tobins had electricity before the electric was anywhere else.

STRAIGHT AS A DIE

Neddy Murphy and Paddy Duggan, both now gone, were having their usual pub argument in Crissey Sheehy's pub, Ballylooby. The topic was who could make the straightest drills for potatoes. Paddy Duggan according to himself was the best, because he was at it since the famine. Little Neddy said….I saw drills that you did and I saw a rabbit rounding the bend and running into a bucket. These two characters were always sparring, it was harmless fun. Talking about wars and soldiering one night back in 1985, a young man asked Paddy if he had seen action, Paddy was about 80 years old at this juncture and was no more than 5 feet tall with bad legs he said that he had a horse shot under him. Little Neddy said you must have been sleeping over a stable at the time.

Neddy, about the same stature as his sparring partner, could not walk without the aid of two sticks. He was just about mobile but he made his way through the fields by way of a mass path to the pub a distance of more than a mile. Neddy lived near Whitechurch with his sister and both were getting on in age. Neddy had a cant of ,,I won't tell you..instead of I don't know, everybody knew this but when Little Neddy ended up in Clonmel Hospital for the first time in his long life, the doctor asked him if he had a medical card…his answer… I won't tell you….

ARMY DEAFNESS

Between 1992-96 there were claims by the defence forces and the temporary militia, of deafness caused by the lack of hearing protection supplied by the Ministry of Defence. The claims cost the country 300 million. Anyone that put on a uniform had a claim. There were 16,971 claims by Oct 2007. Some people were a bit doubtful about others who claimed to have been in the armed forces. A few of us were discussing the situation and Tom said that he heard that a man called Christy told him he was in the army … .Arthur said ..which side was he on.

BERRIHERT'S WELL

This well is on the Aherlow road out of Cahir and is the most unusual of all the Holy Wells, on approach there is a semblance of building containing small gravestones that are placed on the wall for safe keeping. All these pieces date from the 6-9 century. The Kyle contains an amount of children's graves, before going down to the well. A strong spring of water forming a pond 1.5 metres deep and 20 metres across. you can see the crystal clear water bubbling up through the sandy bottom. Around the year 664 St Berrihert arrived from England he was a saxon cleric, following the Synod of Whitby.

SPORTSMEN AND WOMEN

The first Tipperary Women's Gaelic Football Final winners was captained by Kitty Savage { Ryan } from Ardfinnan and was played in Durrow, in 1974.

The second Tipperary Women's Gaelic Football Final Winners was captained by Margaret Rossiter [Carroll] from Cahir in 1975. in Athy.

The Irish Women's Soccer Team has Eileen Miles [Doyle] of Ballylooby who played in goal for Ireland. Eileen has 2 caps and played in the Netherlands and Wembley. In 1987-88.

Another Ardfinnan woman is Nell Carroll who has been capped for Ireland. The same year as Eileen.

Ronan Casey Ginchy Terrace mountain Road. aged 27 years old. Gold Medal in China in two grades. Tug of war. Won Gold in the 680kg club finals National team for the Republic of Ireland.

John Moroney Clogheen Rugby Player. Attended Rockwell and won The Munster Schools. He played for Munster and scored the decisive try that beat Australia in 1967.

Patsy Ward, acknowledged as Cahir Park's best ever player, Patsy played in Colchester and played for Limerick as well as playing for the under 21 National team. Gaining him a Cap John Burke, Mountain Road, Captained Ireland 1928 Played for the Park and Shamrock Rovers.

Ned Tobin Rehill, Ballylooby 56 lb weight thrower Won several National titles. Won first at Fermoy in 1934.

Ger Hawkins who trained more children football, than anybody in Cahir.

OSCAR

Real name Michael Elmer from Emily, Michael came to Ballylooby to work in Crissy Sheehy's pub and yard. He slept in a shed at the rear of the pub. Some of the locals made it habitable. He was popular with all in the village. One of his misfortunes was that he was accident prone. He broke his leg and had it in plaster. He needed to go to the dentist in Clogheen and his only way over there was by bike. On his return to the pub he announced to all..that it was possible to cycle from Clogheen to Ballylooby in 24 mins with one leg. This popular man was killed in a traffic accident on the Cahir road.

MILKMEN

Where did all the milkmen go? When I was a lad we had men who delivered milk in churns on a pony trap or in the boot of the car. The Cooper O'Neills, Tommy, Michael and Noreen on their way to school delivered milk in sweet gallons John Walsh of Sraid Na Gcuic out of the churn, Mattie Martin, Ballydrehid and later his son Seamus. Lonergans the pound on the Clonmel road had boys and girls delivering after school. Going back to the 60s Cahir Park farms had a horse and milk float driven by a man from Kilcommon called Fitzgerald..Bengurrah House farm did deliveries in bottles. Pasteurisation was introduced and sounded the death knell for real milk.

THE HUCKSTER SHOP

All The little shops died a death with the advent of Supermarkets and larger shops. How many remember Mrs Bradley, St.Marys road, Gilley Aherne Church St, Edie Roche Old Church St, .Billie Roche Lower Abbey St, Mrs Devereaux Abbey St, Paddy Franklin Pierce St. Winnie Noone Bridge St, Dan Crowley Upper Abbey St, The Handy Shop, Tipp Road... Mary Annes The Square..Quinns, St Marys Road. Mary Butlers Castle Street, Peggy Chilcots Halpins, Derrygrath.and Matt Hickeys Castle Street, Mulcahy's, The Square.

Crokes ,Castle Street, Kennedys opened the first Supermarket at the top of the Square.

CLOGHEEN MARTYR

Fr. Sheehy was accused of killing a man that was in Newfoundland at the time of the accusation. The Judge handled the trial very badly. But at the end he asked the jury to return an acquittal verdict. The jury returned a verdict of guilty and the Reverend was sentenced to be hanged, drawn and quartered. Two other men were being held in Gaol, they were Ned Meehan and Edmond Sheehy. Ned Meehan was offered his freedom if he would give evidence against the Priest….he would not.

On 15 March 1766 Fr.Sheehy was hanged at Clonmel on a scaffold across the road from St.Paul's Church. His head was severed and put on a spike over Clonmel Gaol for 10 years .

On the 3rd May 1766 Ned Meehan and Edmond Sheehy faced the hangman for being associated with Fr. Sheehy.

His body was eventually buried in Shanrahan cemetery just outside Clogheen. The Lawyer for the defence said ... .if there is any justice in Heaven you will all die roaring.Legend has it that while the priest's head was over the Gaol the birds never pecked it.

BALLYPOREEN

Ballyporeen,the town of the little spud, and is famous for the birthplace of Ronald Reagan's forebears. The complete inside of the pub in Ballyporeen that was named after the American President has been shipped to the United States. The population of the village in 1881 was 632, This was 35 years after the famine. Ballyporeen was originally built by the Kingston family, by a charter from the reigning King. The purpose was to have a military encampment there. To prevent the onset of clansmen or royalty but most of all the reason was to protect the interests of the Kingston's themselves. However The Military never took up residence there and the houses and lands were let to the natives or locals. It is said that they got a good deal. Originally some sort of temporary lease at a very low rate. 4-5 shilling a year for three houses and a bit of land. In law the letting is known as The Ballyporeen Title. The main buildings in the village were intended for the officers and their families. They were later used for an Inn and Hotel, and when Bianconi's coaches were on the road these were now official halts for the changing of the horses and food and refreshments. It is said that the song known as The Wedding of Ballyporeen was composed by John Philpot Curran the father of the fiancee of Robert Emmett.

Curran was going from Dublin to Cork, he was travelling with other students, they broke the journey at the Inn, and on arrival they were informed that the waiter and waitress were to be married that night. The students went out into the street and invited everyone that they saw .Hence the words of the song ,,Tinkers and Tailors, Soldiers and Sailors were all at the wedding at Ballyporeen.

Outside the village in the townland of Kilcaroon stands the Whitethorn tree now famous as the Fairy Tree of Clogheen. The legend about this tree is that at the time of the Danes that were on the run, they buried treasure under the Fairy Tree and that they killed locals and buried them with the treasure, because the Fairies would now guard the Gold. The Song says,,,,,Men and Women passing will turn their heads away.

Another man worthy of a mention was Mick Meaney from Ballyporeen who broke the world record for being buried alive in 1968. Amid great fanfare with all the famous British artists trying to get in on the act. Kilburn in the backyard of a pub was the venue..Diana Dors was there and Jack Doyle sang a few songs. His hero Henry Cooper and half of Tipperary called to see him. The world media was watching. There was a link to America where the American Mr White went down the same day. When asked what he ate, he says that all he wants is steak and a few cigarettes. He never told his wife or daughter because the daughter said that the wife would not allow him. White came up after 55 days but Mick stayed for 6 days more. He was promised everything to stay down. but when he came up he got very little. Mick passed away in Mitchelstown.

The 13th Battalion in the remains of the British Barracks.

SPORT

Kevin O Sullivan Kilcommon. Cahir has the distinction of having in Karate, 3 National Black Belts. One European Medal gained in Portugal,

World bronze medal gained in the Republic of South Africa and a World Bronze Medal from Jakarta Indochina.

Clogheen was the home of two brothers that played for their Country in the years from 1935 to 1948 International football players they were Con and George Moulson. From opposite Lios Mhuire The Mighty Mac, came from Barrack St. and was on the Tipperary team in Croke Park on Bloody Sunday. Jimmy McNamara played on that fateful day in 1920. Jimmy also played with Cahir Park and was offered a place with Glasgow Celtic at £8 a week He refused.

Another man in the Cahir area was Tommy Ryan from Ballylooby that was in Croke Park on that day in 1920..Tommy said…I was about to take a free kick when the machine guns opened up….

John Lonergan of Tubrid won a stage of the Ras Tailteann he beat a Russian champion. The Family were known as Lonergan the Cyclists as all the boys were taking to the handlebars. His brother Joe the Yank from Ardfinnan was another that excelled himself. He won a stage in Castleisland. John Cummins was another Ras contender.

Cooldevane Clogheen was the home of Seamus Durack, a successful Jockey and is now Training in England. For several seasons he was part of the National hunt riders in Ireland and England.

Tommy O'Connors of Ballylooby Castlegrace Gaa club was another that was in Croke Park in November 1920

THE FEAR

Michael Hyland from near Clogheen told me this story a long time ago. Back In the 50s a neighbouring farmer had half his herd of cattle

killed when they were struck by lightning. As was the custom at that time a deputation was chosen to visit the farmers in the vicinity and try to raise enough cash for the herd to be replaced. This was before phones and none of them had a car. They walked through the fields and days were long and they walked well into the night. One evening at dusk they approached Grubb's of Castlegrace and out of the gloom came four men, Mr Grubb was standing by the bridge staring at the four. They walked up to Mr Grubb and explained their plight. The man of the Grubb's collapsed onto the bridge and said almost breathless…..

I thought ye were coming to get me.

STING LIKE A BEE

Mohammed Ali also known as Cassius Clay came to Croke Park on 19 July 1972. He was to fight Al Blue Lewis at the Dublin venue. David Power was a teacher in Rockwell College, and Quiz participant.He needed to train beforehand and several Irish boxers were to warm him up. David Power of Deravoher Ballylooby went two rounds with the Greatest Fighter of all time and lived to tell the tale.

DUHILL CHURCH

Recorded as Castlegrace the windows are actually in Duhill Church. Harry Clarke was without fear of contradiction the foremost stained glass artist in the world. These panels were installed in the church at each side of the altar in 1925.

The scenes depicted are the beheading of John the Baptist and the apparition at Lourdes. Harry had to come down from Dublin to get paid as the Priest at the time was refusing to pay, he said that the scene of the Beheading was too gory. Harry said try cutting off someone's head without blood. The Cleric paid up. Harry passed away in 1931 and left a beautiful legacy in his work.

SLATTERY ROSES

Paddy Slattery came from Rehill Road and his wife Margaret was from Rehill Corner. Not a long way from each other. Pat in his early days got involved with New Ireland Assurance and was with the insurance business all his life. The New Ireland Assurance company was founded by Michael Collins himself. Pat had so much promise that the Insurance sent him to Third Level education. After moving around the country he was finally sent to Dundalk where he got interested in rose growing and was influenced by the famous Sam McGready the master. Pat and his family moved back to Rehill where the rose business flourished.He Swapped the land in Rehill for the land in Cahir Park. This was done in hand with the land commission. Pat also had another outlet, the Kilcoran garden centre, where his sister lived. Slattery's Roses were known all over the country and employed twenty workers at times. Pat was full time gardening but found time to write several books about the locality. He was involved in the erection of several monuments, notably the Tobin monument in Ballylooby village. No doubt the greatest achievement of his was the Kilcoran New Burgess group water scheme in the early 60s. The well is to be found at the Kilcoran Garden Centre. This was great foresight with 120 shareholders on the scheme. Pat played no small part in the erection of the Geoffrey Keating Monument At Burgess.

TUBRID

Every year for as long as people remember in Tubrid Church very large birds called Peregrine Falcons, have made their nest and have bred there, these large birds are not to be approached.

PARK AVENUE

Where Park Avenue is now, at the rear of Cahir House Hotel, there used to be a Tennis Court and a Bowling Green as well as a Croquet Lawn..

There was also a showroom belonging to Burkes of Ford Garages where the new Anglia was launched.

PADDY O SULLIVAN

Paddy O Sullivan arrived in Cahir with his Amusements and never left. His family are mostly in Cahir. Paddy and his wife Aggie had a long and happy life together. One of the pubs that he frequented was Michael Meads on Barrack St. This was the time when pubs had characters and Meadoes was not short. Many strange topics were often discussed. That night, it was long livers. Someone asked Paddy if his family lasted a long time. The lie came straight away without blinking he went on to relate that his grandfather would be still alive only for the poteen. Meado asked if he had a problem, Paddy replied no….he had a bad back. What has a bad back got to do with living long? Paddy said that it was the vet's fault because he rubbed poteen into his back and grandad broke his neck trying to lick it off.

ABBEY SERVICE GARAGE

For a start it is not a garage, it is a tool shop and industrial gas supplier.

Captain Beary, always called Captain, set the business in motion shortly after the Emergency. Pat Beary, his son, now runs the show. Pat and myself went to school together and lived on Abbey St. We are both in the

Mid 70s. One day I went in to buy an electric drill only to be told that I should not buy anything electric at my age.

HIDDEN WELL

Underneath the Blind Piper in the Square, the County Council were digging to improve the Plaza in front of the Market House [library].When the ground gave way and the discovery of an ancient well was uncovered. A perfect circle of cut stone and was about 80 ft, deep a masterpiece in its day. The well was there a long time before the fountain, but it was covered over because of the cholera epidemic at the time. There was fear that the graveyard at the old church was the cause of the well being infected. So when those that love a crown tell you that Mag. Charteris was the first to give water to the people of the town. Remind them of the ancient well.

MORE SPORT

Tommy O Donnell started playing rugby with Clanwilliam and then went

On to Munster, he played international rugby for Ireland. He retired in 2021 with 13 caps for his country.

Strength and Conditioning coach Paudie Roche Holds a masters degree from Edith Cowan University. Before going to England he was Conditioning coach to The Munster rugby and Ireland National rugby team he was awarded the coach of the year in 2015 by UKSCA. With Arsenal he is Head coach to the Arsenal womens and mens under 23 and under 18s squads.

Whenever Camogie is mentioned in Cahir one name comes to the fore all the time, Kitty O Flaherty was the name that stands out, she was from Market Street and loved by everyone.

All Ireland medal winner at Handball, a man from Ballyporeen called Gummy Gorman, lost his medal in a field and some 35 years later it was found and returned to his daughter.

Aishling Moloney, All Ireland Intermediate Footballer of the Year. She won an Intermediate Camogie club All Ireland with Cahir in Croke Park.

Paddy Saunders started playing with Ballylooby Castlegrace but moved to Cahir where he Captained Cahir to 3 County Titles in 1953-55-58.

Couldn't play for Munster due to suspension.

Kevin Lafford of New Inn, Munster Rivers Fishing Champion in 2022..Munster Banks Champion..2016-2019…Gold Medal with the Irish team 2022 in Wales…Heaviest fish trophy in Scotland…Won the team event in the Munster rivers competition in Cahir 2024.

Ned Tobin of Rehill Ballylooby, discus and 56 lb weight thrower. He won 37 national titles and was known as the Tipperary Giant. 6ft 5in.

ELECTION BLUES

He is known for many things but he called himself Doctor Martin, Anthony Francis O' Halloran and he was my Director of elections, two out of three successes. We completed the campaigns without killing each other, This is one of the reasons that I wanted to do him an injury. I eventually topped the poll in the Cahir area in the 2009 local elections. Because we were getting a good response at the doors Our mood was good.

The good Doctor does not drive and he does not have a mobile phone, he had to be delivered and brought home at the end of the day. The next day was going to be a busy one as we had to meet Pat Rabbite to help us for an afternoon canvass.

Night Time and I dropped him off at his home in Ardfinnan and warned him to be up out of bed when I called in the morning.

Morning I called to his home in Ardfinnan and his Mother answered the door. Is he up? ..I asked . His mother said that he did not come home the night before. But she added this is not unusual, He would often go to his sister Vanessa and bed down there, it is getting late so I drive to his sister's house in Ardfinnan, Vanessa says she did not see him, maybe he was gone to his other sister Clare, who was in Cahir. He did not have a mobile phone, he used mine. I drove to Clare's house and lo and behold she had no idea where he was, maybe he was gone to his sister Olivia who lived halfway to Mitchelstown. Time was running out, I drove to Olive's.... no sign.

I pulled into the side of the road, my head spinning and I rang my wife Mag, was there any call from that bastard O Halloran?.

Her answer haunts me for the rest of my life…will I call him she asked…

What do you mean call him ? He is upstairs in the spare room…..

I was driving all round the country and he is upstairs in my own house. Seems he met some friends the night before and they went for a drink and he made his way to my house at 5 am and let himself in.

As Van Morrisson sang, My Momma told me that there would be days like this.

GENERAL WILLIAM FRANCIS BUTLER

William Francis Butler was born in Ballyslateen Golden he was son of Richard Butler of Ballycarron Cahir. One of his earliest memories is visiting Daniel O Connell in Richmond prison with his father. William travelled the world with the British army, on his way home from one of his trips he visited Napoleon's Tomb in St.Helena. He knew Victor Hugo and Hugo asked him to be his guide when he came to Ireland.

In 1867 he was sent to Canada, to help prevent a Fenian invasion. that never happened. He was sent on a roving mission around Saskatchewan before the new orders came that he was to trek from Quebec to the Rockies a distance of 4345 km.

After this expedition he was to recommend the formation of a roving mounted police force that evolved into the Mounties. The RCMP. That was in 1871 the year that he was promoted to Captain. He returned to London to be told that he was being sent on an expedition to North America. William traversed the land that was occupied by the native American people. Travelling by foot, dog sled, horse and canoe.

Later he published accounts of his adventures…The Great Lone Land..and The Wild North Land. He greatly admired the courage and tenacity of the Native Americans and after returning he wrote two more books Red Cloud and The Solitary Sioux.

He succumbed to fever that he contracted on his travels and spent 2 months in hospital but as soon as he was well enough he was posted to Africa for the Zulu war, following the war he was promoted to Lieutenant Colonel, and was posted to Egypt in 1882, this was a quiet posting and he found time to write, he wrote …The invasion of England..foretelling of things to come by Germany.

Whitehall regarded him as a trouble maker as well as being Irish and a Catholic to boot. He befriended many of the Irish insurgents and notably used to go shooting with Charles Steward Parnell in 1888, He admired Parnell as a decent political leader and he befriended John Redmond before returning to Egypt. He was buried with full military honours at Kilalldriffe .Kilmoyler, Cahir. at the foot of the Galtees.

He married Elizabeth Thompson and they had three sons and two daughters. His wife Lady Elizabeth Butler was in her own right a very famous and talented artist, she painted works such as ... .The Roll Call ... .The Charge of the Light Brigade and lots more.

Elizabeth was the doyen of London aristocracy …until she painted a work called The Eviction…this work was of a woman standing beside her roofless cottage and was heart wrenching. The despicable aristocracy did not want to be reminded how things were in Ireland because they were all absent landlords and all they wanted was rent coming in.

Elizabeth died in 1933 and is buried at Gormanston.

NOT ON ANY MAP

You won't find The Reiska Road on any map because it is a name used only by locals, some say that it means Kings Water or wet place.

Nor will you find the Khyber Pass in Cahir on any map.

Jude Noggins road is out by Rehill but on no map.

The Road of the Corpses is from the famine times From Cahir to Clogheen. So called because the work was too hard and the starving people were not able to do it.

Until 2009 Sraid Na Gcuic was not official until Councillor Lonergan asked the Council to name the New houses with the old name.

How many people know where the Lacka is?. It is at the rear of the Protestant Church and at the end of the Mall.

The Cover is in Garryclogher and is an animal sanctuary that used to belong to Cahir Estates. Now it belongs to Coillte..

Seanie Lonergan

AN EMIGRANTS FAREWELL TO CLOGHEEN

By JOHN DALY

Dear native land by fate's cruel hand,
I am forced across the wave,
To toil for gold from strangers cold,
Or to find an exiles grave,
No more i'll climb in Summer time,
Thy sides, tall Knockmealdown,
While bright green trees play with the breeze,
In the groves round Clogheen town.

No more I'll stray at break of day,
On the banks of lone Baylough,
Nor free from care pursue the hare,
Through Bohernagore and Crough,
Ah,happy years with longing tears,
From many an alien scene,
My thoughts will fly to times gone by,
And the groves round dear Clogheen.

By Shan'ran's Tower at the midnight hour,

I knelt in the old Churchyard

To pray God Rest those I love best,

Who now sleep beneath the sward,

Peace they have found, in this hallowed ground,

Where spirits may rove unseen,

But I must go , in grief and woe,

From the graves near dear Clogheen.

One last goodbye to Ballyboy

To Garrymore and Bohergore

To Graigue and Castlegrace,

To the bridge and River Screen

With breaking heart I will depart,

From thy groves dear dear Clogheen.

SHORTS

Before Coillte we had the Forestry Commission and there was plenty of employment, every day there was a troop of workers heading for the mountain. Two men that I remember were Paddy Ryan and Jim Mulkearns, with their Honda 50s and the terriers on the seat behind them. Yes, bringing their dogs to work.

The Dovecote on the Park walk, all the big houses and Castles had pigeon houses, apart from bringing messages the birds were used to make Pigeon Pies and fed the rich and poor. The quaker houses on the Tipperary Road had dovecotes built into the Main house.

Just down a piece from the dovecote is the Castle ice house, this is an underground room that, during the winter, the inhabitants shovelled snow and ice into it. During the Summer the underground would be cool and food could be stored there.

The night the Black and Tans went on a rampage, not only did they blow up Tincurry House, they destroyed 11 more that night. Here are six more in the Cahir area. Dwyers Ballydavid Mulcahy's near the caves Keatings Ballylooby, James Slattery, Kilbeg, Tom O'Gorman Burncourt and Mccarthy's ...Drumlemmin.

In the magically named Clogheenapisogue, the little stone of the Fairies. There is a field that has a Bulaun stone almost in the centre, the stone has five Bullauns which is most unusual and like all ancient stones it is reputed to have healing powers. Warts again is the ailment that it cures. Local folklore suggests that the stone was used as a mass rock. There is a legend attached to the rock and it has, that a man was ploughing the field and he caught the plough in the stone breaking a small piece. One of the neighbours told him that he would have nothing but bad luck from there on. The poor man went away and took his own life. Such was the fear of pishogues. [fairy magic].

TIMMY LOONEY

Timmy Looney was born in Cahir in 1914. A well known historian, he could regularly be found exploring castles, churches, graveyards and sites of historical interest. He was known to question established beliefs and traditions and to use evidence of elements such as documents and landscapes to offer alternative interpretations. His house on Pearce Street, a treasure trove of maps, books, documents and photographs, was a popular port of call for genealogists tracing their ancestors and for scholars researching historical topics. Timmy's collecting activities culminated in a remarkable salvage operation to recover papers from Shanbally Castle, Clogheen, County Tipperary, prior to its destruction by a controlled explosion in March 1960.

In addition to his historical pursuits, Timmy was an active member of his local community. He had a lifelong interest in the

GAA and was influential in the development of Gaelic games in Cahir. He was a tireless charity worker and fundraiser, throughout the 1950s and 1960s. He organised volunteers to travel around the country to collect funds for the Central Remedial Clinic, known as the Little Willie Fund, to aid the plight of polio victims. A supporter of the Trade Union Movement he was also active in The Irish Transport and General Workers Union. He had a great fondness for Cahir and campaigned prominently to save the Railway Station. Timmy passed away in Cahir 1990. The documents relating to Shanbally Castle were salvaged by Timmy in 1960 as the building was being prepared for demolition. All his manuscripts and other files were donated to the University of Limerick by Timmy's family

Mary Johannes, Kathleen Muir, Helen O'Sullivan and John Looney.

P.J. Duggan of Lochloher was a colleague of Timmy's for a number of years This was the same Timmy Looney that bought the Whorts at the wood gate all those years ago….. Thanks to the University of Limerick.

SHEILA NA GIG

There is a Sheila Na Gig in Shanrahan church in Clogheen; it is high up on the tower wall for safekeeping. The church is Catholic or Christian but the effigy is a pagan sculpture and by right it should not be there. The non Christians were reluctant to let the old beliefs go. So to play safe they brought their old ways with them. The Sheila Na Gig is a fertility symbol dating back thousands of years. There are two more effigy's hidden in the Graveyard.

Laura McCraith from Lochloher wrote a book in 1912 called ... .The Suir From its Source to the Sea..complete with photographs by Philip Condon of Church Street. When it was published it received great acclaim as the most informative of its kind ever published in Tipperary.

During the British occupation at the army barracks in 1914. There was an officer who was wooing a girl from Kilcommon. He was being posted overseas and asked for her hand in marriage, she was not ready to be wed and she said that she would wait, if he gave her a token, ensuring his return. He gave her his sword and she took it for safekeeping...He never returned, killed in action......The sword is still in that house today.

TURF TO CLOGHEEN POORHOUSE

There is a high bog above Mount Anglesby in Clogheen and the road up to it is called Dan Cookes road. Dan used to deliver the turf down to the Poorhouse, as he was the only one that had a truck in those days. The turf was free to the poor in the early 40s .To the Poorhouse at least.

The Hospital now stands where the poorhouse was and the road is now called the Convent Road, it used to be the pound road. The Ormond Cinema was also on this road and dances were held there when the cinema closed in 1954.

SHORTS

In Jack Briens hall even though it was inside, there was a stage in days gone by.Goatenbridge was the venue for the dances that attracted very large crowds. A local woman said that she and her friends would go early and Brien's always had a pig's head already cooked before the hooley. They would have their fill of boiled pig's head and cabbage before the music started.

Still in Goatenbridge, Majella Carrigan has in her possession a necklace that was made from a silver spoon, while her father was in Clonmel prison. The man that made it was a Jeweller, who was incarcerated with all the rest of the rebels and made it for Majellas mother, a present from her father in prison, in 1921.

Garryroan Cahir. There were tailors in the townland in the 1900s they were called Richardsons and were known far and wide. There was a huge sycamore tree beside their house and every weekend, old man Richardson would climb halfway up it and play the bagpipes. Often people would dance to the music. They never married and the family died out. Folklore has it that there were about 12 taylors employed there and were known all over Munster.

CAHIR GAA

Their present location is in place since the Cahir Estate broke up in 1961. The first trustees John O Donnell, Timmy Looney.and Donnacha Long. Before that the Slashers as they were known, played at Clonmore/Glen Righ. The club has been going, some say, since around 1885. The same year as the GAA was founded. The first secretary of the first committee was Frank English from Garryroan. In 2010 the Cahir Ladies went on to win the National title. The men won the County Senior Football Championships. They have a host of successes in all grades and ages .

HARD TO MAKE A LIVING

Tommy lived on the Tipperary road and times were tough back in the 1960s ,it was almost impossible to meet the repayments on a bank loan. The rate was at times 17.5% and the banks had no mercy. Our Tommy was a small farmer and pigs were his mainstay. Tommy worked like a dog but was getting nowhere. The bank manager called him into his office to discuss the matter. The manager told Tommy…the only way to get out of this predicament was to borrow more money and invest in more pigs ... ..Tommy asked the Bank manager…do you know much about pigs ?. The man says not a lot. Says Tommy you better learn fast because you have 300 pigs to feed tomorrow. I'm off to England.

HAPPY CHRISTMAS

In 1965 there was a big cleanup at St.Mary's Cemetery in the main part. When all the earth and general rubbish was removed there were about 100 or so new grave spaces created. These were sold to the Cahir people for the going rate of that time, which was £5. Bridie Lonergan purchased 3 at the time. One for herself and one each for her son and daughter. I am her son and a few days before Christmas I went up home and my mother had my Christmas present ready, a box with a pair of boots and a receipt for a grave, and that's all you are getting, she said.

Some people might think this a little unusual, not if you knew my mother.

THE 12TH DAIL

William O Donnell of Clonmore was elected to the 12th Dail in 1943 for the Clann Na Talmhan party in County Tipperary. Following a short tenure he was reelected in 1944. He was prolific in his quest for rural water supplies which were non-existent, he was so insistent that one chairman accused him of having water on the brain. On the night of his election a man rode a horse wildly around the countryside and into every yard ..shouting he's elected..he's elected. William passed away in 1947.

SUIRVALE HOUSE

Once called Abbey View and also known as Jellicoe's because at one time it was owned by the Quaker Jellicoe family. Maggie and Brendan Davis were previous owners, their daughter is the opera singer Jennifer Davis. Before them in no particular order were artist Monica Duckworth and her daughter Scarlet. A Mr. and Mrs. Gardiner who kept Jacob Sheep. Going back before 1980 there was a General Harris from Ballykisteen who was responsible for disbanding the B Specials in the north of Ireland. Midway through the 20th century the name Lord Jellicoe was caught up in a scandal that came to be known as the Profumo Affair. Harold McMillan the British Prime Minister resigned and among the other resignations was Jellico. This scandal brought down the Government. At the time that the Cahir Catholic Church was being built the Clergy were housed here. During the British occupation British Officers stayed at this house. One misfortunate lodger was Private Kenny [Kreutz] who was hanged in Clonmel for killing a fellow soldier at the British Army Barracks Cahir.

TOBINS OF TINCURRY

Marian Tobin was a staunch member of Cumann Na Mban, but her family were not of the same persuasion. Marian's cousin was a Doctor Tobin who spoke out in the House of Commons about the behaviour of the Black and Tans, when they destroyed Tincurry House. Frank Tobin Wall, Paymaster, was killed when his ship HMS Triumph was torpedoed off the Dardanelles May 1915. John Tobin Willis Lieutenant, RFC, killed in action France 1917. Marian's husband James was a Captain in the Irish Volunteers, he passed away in 1918. Marian died in Sept,1955 aged 84.

THE WAR MEMORIAL

The memorial is often mistaken for honouring the British war dead only. All the names inscribed are from Cahir and the surrounding areas. The cost was borne by the local people. The monies raised were from public subscription. The monument honours all those that died in any conflict. It was unveiled in 1930. We cannot talk about this edifice without a mention of Johnny O Brien who looked after the flowers and took care of it for so many years. Johnny took care of it when he was well into his 90s. Almost all of us Cahir people have a relation who is connected to the fallen. A few years ago some officials wanted to move it to the rear of the car park, there was a public outcry and it remains.

GALTEE HOTEL

March 2024 saw the last of an Iconic building when the County Council had the Galtee Hotel taken down, to put extra parking for the town. Once a hub and a decent hotel. When the last owner abandoned it, the vandals moved in and burned most of the building. It became an eyesore and had to be demolished. Before it was a hotel it was a clergyman's house and was purchased by the Kennedy family who enlarged the frontage. I can remember when the Cahir Lions Club had fundraisers there, a hundred tables or so for the Quiz. Gerry Kelly of the ESB used to organise 25 drives and there would be 100 tables again. Dances and Socials were the order of the day. I remember managers such as Joan Lonergan and Jim Nolan who were well respected.

HOLLOWAY

Directly across from the Post Office is Looby and McCarthy's former offices. It used to be Holloways Pub and grocer shop, the man that built the Post Office. He also had a hand later in the building of the Church and had some marble left over. He incorporated the marble into his shop front. The Priest completely lost the plot and castigated him from the pulpit. The lords stone outside a den of iniquity, damnation.

LIAM LYNCH

Liam Lynch was an Irish Republican Army officer during the War of Independence 1919-1921. His rank was Chief of Staff of the Irish Republican Army. On the 10th April 1923. He was crossing the foothills of the Knockmealdown Mountains above Goatenbridge, he was in uniform and with several comrades and carrying a rifle. The Free State Army was closing in. Lynch told his comrades to save themselves.He was on the townland of Crohan when a shot rang out from long distance and hit Liams lower chest, the Free State Soldiers ran to where he lay and one said ..we got Dev..Lynch said I am not Dev get me a Priest and a doctor I am dying. They brought him down to Houlihans house where he had his wounds dressed and had a bite to eat. On their way down the mountain and heading for Newcastle, they stopped at ... .Sheehans formerly Burkes ...Where Father Hallinan anointed him.and then they went to Nugent's Pub. That night in Clonmel hospital Liam Lynch passed away. He is buried in Kilcrumper old Churchyard.

On the 7th April 1935 there was a 60ft round tower unveiled on the spot where he was shot on the lonely wooded slopes of Crohan Mountain.

How different would Ireland be if it was Dev. that was shot.?

MAURICE CONDON

Down all the days that the train entered the station there was the figure of a man with a cigarette in the side of his mouth, shouting Hostel. Hostel. He had a hikers hostel on the Ardfinnan road. He and his wife ran a shop across from the Post Office. He was a famous Cahir wit and one of the stories was when he played football for the Slashers. A terribly wet day and both teams were in the tiny shed changing. The ref was in with the teams and attempting to toss. He tossed the coin and Maurice won. He was asked what direction he wanted. We'll play with the tide..he says.

It used to be said that he was the only man that could whistle with a cigarette in his mouth.

DOROTHEA HERBERT

Born in Carrick On Suir in 1767 Dorothea moved to Knockgraffon when her father, a Minister of religion, was given a new ministerial posting.

Dorothea wrote several diaries which were later published in book form.

Retrospections of an Outcast for instance, is the dramatic title of a memoir written by Dorothea, whose experience of mental illness formed the central drama in her life. Despite this she was able to use her talent for writing and painting to produce plays and poetry as well as novels and the illustrated memoir. She had a haphazard education and was lucky to get the sketchy tutoring that she had.: access to education was denied to many girls in the 18th century. We learn from her writings that she learned French and preferred poetry and art to needlework, she loved gardening and practical jokes. Her memoirs are a gold mine as women's records from this age are very rare. Not only does it give details about how it was to live in a not so normal home in the eighteenth century. It also gives an insight into unrecorded activities of children who are usually absent from records from that time.

Dorothea's recollection of games and at that time the children were mostly unsupervised after an attempt was made to educate them like playing Robinson Crusoe with her brothers to dangerous pranks like setting the Music teacher on fire. Herbert describes how she and her friend Betty used to smear themselves with ointment and cover themselves in brown paper to protect their complexion. Her description of her best friend Betty being whisked off against her will to be married is heartbreaking, as her friend was only 15.

The heir to Rockwell at that time was a man called John Roe and was not married. Dorothea's Parents wanted her to marry a young Pastor from Carrick On Suir but Dorothea refused even though she admired her suitor, she only had eyes for John Roe.

The betrayal by Roe caused Dorothea to withdraw from society and the death of her Step mother by the Whiteboys did not help her mental condition.

A TRIP TO AMERICA

Another true story, but the name has to be changed. This man worked in the Cahir Proteins in the 1990s.He informed all of us workers that he was out of this hell hole in a few months. His sister was getting married in America and he was going to the wedding and not coming back. The factory was a very unpleasant place to work as it was a rendering plant for dead animals and offal and the like. The money was good in bad times and Pat would have no trouble in saving up for his fare. Every day he reminded us that he was out of there soon. On his day off he used to go to the Credit Union and purchase dollars for the venture. He showed us all his brand new passport that arrived that morning. For safekeeping he hid the dollars and passport under the stairs in one of the old shoes that there were hundreds of. After two months there was a fair wad of dollars and he would be alright in America. All his family were going including his father and mother. His parents were never out of the country and it was a nervous time for them. Pat's last day at work and he shook hands with us all and we wished him luck.

Monday morning and Pat turned up for work, naturally we were curious and asked about the American trip. In whispered tones and a quiver in his voice he said ... .because of the flying his mother could not sleep and set about tidying the whole house. She gathered all the old shoes from under the stairs and brought them out back and had a bonfire.........

A SAFE PLACE

Cheltenham takes place every year around St.Patrick's day and our Mick was hell bent on going. This man had a different method of taking care of his money. Coming from a large family it would be risky to bring it home. So he got an old biscuit tin and put it in it. Every time he got paid he stashed his cash in the tin and when the time for the crowds to descend on the Cheltenham races Mick was there. While he was there he made the newspapers and the headline was ... .Man hides biscuit tin full of money in family grave for safe keeping....true.

THE HAPPIEST DAYS OF OUR LIVES

To anyone else the happiest days of our lives should have been our school days. Not in the Cahir Boys National School in the early 60s. We had the misfortune of attending when Baldy ruled, he did more damage to the pupils than anyone before or after. It is a very bad reflection that the only part of one's school time memories is the beatings and the terrible insults about families. Anyone that attended at the tyrant's reign will agree with me.How he was allowed to remain as school principal we will never know. After the primary there was a choice of the Tech, or St.Josephs. I was sent to the Tech, where we were taught by the likes of Arthur Carter before his ordination. Liam Simpson and the headmaster was Jimmy Flanagan who ruled the school without any sticks. We could not believe that we were not victims of punishment by slapping with a stick. St. Josephs. At that time it was a fee paying school, I seem to remember that it was £3 per year in the late 50s. Not a lot of money now, back then it was a week's wages.

CAHIR ARTS

Paddy Caplice was a Fianna Fail Councillor and Estate agent and Auctioneer. He and his wife Sadie lived in Kilcommon, their daughter Siobhan married a Frenchman in Ireland and decided to go to Paris, for the next 32 years she divided her time between Paris and Lille. Siobhan was trained as a nurse but ended up teaching English, in between she did photography and the arts. Her marriage did not survive and after her divorce she decided to return and open an art gallery. Siobhan took a giant step and purchased her premises in Castle Street on the computer, online.. She returned in the beginning of 2021 and after a hard slog opened the gallery in 2021. The gallery is a Centre for the promotion of Irish art. Oils and watercolours. Porcelain and any medium you care to mention.

Courses in pottery and lectures all take place in this wonderful outlet.

CONDON'S BAR

Fondly remembered as Archies and as usual being Irish his name was Gerry. It seems that when Gerry went to Rockwell and played rugby, there was an international called Archibald and his schoolmates called him after his idol. As well as a public house they also had a restaurant, It was a busy side of town, as the Undertaking business took a share of his time. At that time he had to make his own coffins which involved carpentry and french polishing, upholstery, all done with hand tools.

Archie Joined the British army and was posted overseas to Italy, Germany, Greece and mastered five languages as he had an ear for the foreign tongue. He returned and took up where he left off. The Condon family were all around Church Street. A Man called Jimmy Johnson started work with the Condons at age 13 and remained to rear 5 generations. Jimmy did most of the Photography with a large box camera on a tripod. The lady that gave me this story is Archie's daughter Mary. Jimmy used to go home across town for his lunch, one day when he returned he found Mary's grandmother dead after complications in childbirth. This had a terrible effect on the man.

Mary's uncle Chris and his wife returned from America following the death of their infant child. Chris had a travel agency beside the Post Office. He was an agent for Cunard and he had a large cardboard cutout of the Titanic in the window. The Titanic was the White Star Line.

He had a petrol pump outside on the footpath. He was a gunsmith selling and repairing arms. His musical endeavours stretched to playing piano and accordion with Kevin Flynn's Band. On top of that he had an Insurance business called Phoenix. All this from a man that was in the United States Army. These were the days when pubs had a character or two, Archies had 100 of them. Ronnie Bearmore…Walter Nolan..Jack Williams..Paud O Shea..Tommy Maher..Ned Harris…Jim Carew..Mickey Mack..Dick Ryan. There was a card game played there that was never seen anywhere else…Napoleon ..a game when played right brought out the lunacy in a man.

DARLING

Paud O Shea came from and I tell no lie, a place called Ballyfookeen next to Nicker in County Limerick. This was the butt of a lot of ribbing as you can imagine. He lived on the Priest's Road in a nice country cottage. Paud called everyone darling as he was bad with names. He had a liking for a pint of stout and sometimes he overdid it. He had to have a walking stick to get around. One night he arrived in the pub without the stick and accused all and sundry of stealing his walking aid.

Jim Coughlan delivered him home that night and the next night he was back in the bar with the stick. Where was the stick asked Archie ?..I found it darling hanging on the gable end of the bed. .was the reply. Pauds brother went to the trouble of paying him a visit coming from Limerick on the bus. Paudie asked the time of the bus returning to Limerick. He did not care for relatives.

Paudie passed away and he had a bit of cash and a house, he also had relations at home in Nicker, they were not happy with the Will arrangements and there was a court case in the Clonmel Circuit Court The hearing was attended by relatives and friends some of which had never been past Ballyfookeen. After about an hour into the case the Judge was surprised to see some of the spectators in the gallery taking out a Thermos Flask and sandwiches and an apple tart and partaking thereof. The Judge did not take kindly to the picnic being held in court. The last will and testament remained unchanged.

THE BRIDE IN A&E

When Mary Condon was getting married to Pat O Connor they had a little mishap. Something borrowed something blue as the saying goes. The wedding party arrived and the guests were in place, Mary and Pat were at the altar. The ambience was broken by a loud groan and a part of the wedding party were in panic. Mary's mother had collapsed.The panic was on, the Bride and Groom rushed her to A&E where Mary spent her wedding day in her wedding dress and missing her honeymoon. The mother recovered after a time.

CAHIR SESSIONS JULY 1912

At Cahir Petty Sessions on Thursday,the magistrates were - Messrs T .Burke, B.L.[presiding] and William, M, Ryan.

Catherine English Tobins Lane, summoned her husband Edward English for using threatening and abusive language,and made an application to have him bound to the peace. She stated he had been drinking for the past seven weeks, and refused to work ; on Monday night last he threatened to kill her.

This the defendant denied, and he called Constable Conway to give a testimonial as to character. The Constable however said that one party was as bad as the other.

On the defendant giving a guarantee to go to work immediately, the case was dismissed with a caution.

Tobias F. Egan, Lisava, summoned William Keyes, Kellys Lane, for the trespass of a jennet and donkey, on a field of oats on various dates.

The defendant at first denied ownership of the animals but on cross examination he admitted it. Complainant said that he did not wish to press the case.

The magistrates commented strongly on the defendant's denial of the ownership, and fined him 6s and 2s.costs.

Constable Mulligan summoned the same defendant for cruelty to an ass, while working it, whilst suffering from a sore on its back; it was stated that the defendant was fined for a similar offence. The defendant pleaded guilty.

The Chairman said that as the defendant had been already fined in a previous case, the court would let him off with a fine of 6d.

The police prosecuted several persons for road nuisance, for which small penalties were imposed.

Constable Rafter prosecuted Eilish Doyle for being drunk and disorderly. fined 5s and 1s costs.

Miss Harvey obtained a decree against Brigid Power for possession of a small tenement in Kelly's Lane, Solicitor appealed for complainant.

CATHOLIC INHABITANTS WHO SWORE OATHS OF ALLEGIANCE TO THE KING.

Leonard Dougherty of Loughloher, Esq.

John Dougherty of Outrath, Esq.

Stephen Egan, Cahir, Merchant.

James Everard of Cahir, Sadler.

Terence Flinn of Cahir, Schoolmaster.

Sylvester Greene, of Cahir, Apothecary.

James Hennessey of Knockgraffon, Surveyor.

Pierce Hickie of Cahir, Innholder.

Michael Kavenagh of Cahir, Victualler.

James Keating of Clogheen, Gent.

Michael Keating of Cahir, Gent.

John Keating of Rehill, Farmer.

Jeffrey Keating, of Cahir, Gent.

Pierce Keating, Knockagh, Esq.

John Kelly of Cahir, Woolcomber.

Michael Kelly of Knockgraffon, Gent .

William Meagher, of Carrigatagh, Esq.

William Meagher of Toureen. Esq.

James Moroney of Cahir, Merchant.

James Murphy of Cahir. Innholder.

William Murphy of Cahir, Master.

Edmond Power of Garnavilla, Esq.

Redmond Power of Lisava, Esq.

Charles Ryan of Kilcommon, Wheelwright.

Walter Stapleton of Cahir, Farmer.

Given under our hands 18th december 1775. James Butler of Kilcommon, Esq. And William Hayes of Lissava, Esq.

Justices of the Peace for the County of Tipperary.

MAN ARRESTED IN CAHIR - LARCENY OF £3 NOTE

Clonmel October 1913.

Yesterday a man of the labouring class called John O Donnell of Mooneraha near Cahir, was arrested by Sergeant Cole on the charge of stealing a £3 note the property of Miss Alice Lonergan, farmer's

daughter of Ballymacadam, Cahir.

Sergeant Cole arrested O'Donnell while in bed at an early hour this morning. On searching O'Donnells clothes the sergeant found a £3 note in one of his pockets.

At a special court in Cahir before Mr. Wm, F Ryan. J.P.; O'Donnell was charged by Mr Potter. D.I. with the larceny of a £3 note from Miss. Lonergan.

Alice Lonergan verified an information given by her before William F, Ryan ,J.P. yesterday evening. She stated that on Monday morning she brought a pig to Cahir for sale. She sold the animal for £3. 13 shillings. and that it was paid by a £3 note: 10 shillings in gold and 3 shillings in silver. She changed the 2 shilling piece and had going home with her the £3 note and 10 shillings in gold and 1 shilling in silver and 6 coppers. Shortly after going home John O'Donnell of Mooneraha came in and asked her what she sold the pig for. Witness said she made £3. 13 shillings. O'Donnell said that he thought it would make more than that.. she should have made £4…In O'Donnell's presence she put the Money into her purse and left the purse on a shelf on the dresser. She then went to tackle the donkey to go to Cahir for some Groceries. When she had the donkey tackled and ready to start she went in for the purse and missed the £3 note. She then asked O'Donnell who was in the house the whole time , where was the £3 note ?.O'Donnell said : you did not put it into it, you might have swept it into the fire : She said that she did not sweep it into the fire. O'Donnell said that he did not know that she put the note into her purse, and she said that she did. O'Donnell then started to look around for it…he then left the house and crossed the fields in the direction of the house where her uncle John Lonergan lived.

Witness came to Cahir and reported the matter to her uncle Matthew Lonergan at the Convent and later on in the evening she told the police about it. Witness added that before O'Donnell left her house he said to her : I will be in a holy show over this and he then cautioned her about telling anybody.: He told me, said the witness, not to even let the ground know for if I told anyone, myself would be the laughing stock of all the people. He then turned pale and took a cup of water. There was nobody in the house, only O'Donnell and I firmly believe it was he who took the money. He saw me put the money in the purse and nobody could have taken it.

Cross examined by the prisoner–Did I take the money ?. Nobody was in the house, only yourself. Did you show me the money ?

She…yes you took the £3 in your hand and said that you thought it was £1.note.

Did I hand it back to you? Witness Yes and I put it in the purse.

Didn't I go and look for the money „yes and you said that I had a hole in my pocket and I said that I did not put it in my pocket

Did I say to you that you would blame me for the money?….Yes there was nobody else in the house.

Did I tell you to search me before I left the house ?… You did.

Sergeant Cole deposed that he obtained a search warrant on Monday night to search the house where the prisoner resided with his father.

This morning about 7 o'clock he saw the prisoner sitting undressed on the side of the bed. Witness said : I suppose you know why I am here. Prisoner said ..no.. Witness then said that he had come about the £3 note; Prisoner said is that Alice Lonergans? Witness said yes..Prisoner said I was there but I didn't take it. Witness then directed the prisoner to dress himself. The prisoner's trousers were lying on the floor and when he was in the act of putting them on the witness searched the pockets and in one of them he found the purse. The purse contained nothing, only the £3 note, which the witness now produced.

Witness asked him if he could account for his possession of the note and he replied that he had been saving up for a long time to enable him to go to America. Witness pressed him as to the person from whom he received it. The prisoner said that he got it in the Post Office about three months ago..Witness then arrested him and charged him with stealing the note from Miss Lonergan.

On the application of Mr. Potter the prisoner was remanded.

Mr. Ryan J.P. said he would allow bail—two sureties of £10 each.

The prisoner did not apply for bail.

This is the same Mr Potter that Dan Breen and others captured and killed.

MURDER OF AN EVICTED FARMER

Cahir 1892

A murder of a strange character has just been committed in Cahir.It appears that a farmer named Quirke, of Ballybacon, near Ardfinnan,went on friday to the house of an evicted farmer named Patrick Doolan who lived by himself in a small house, and finding the door closed with some obstruction, he pushed it in and found Doolan stretched dead near the door in a pool of blood. He immediately reported the matter to the police, who visited the place and discovered that the unfortunate man's skull was broken an discovered a large hammer and a washerwomans beadle in which there were human hair and blood marks were lying covenant .They searched the house and discovered no money even though they believed that the murdered man must have had some. As he got nearly £6 , the amount of a decree obtained at the last assizes and it was known that he got some other monies lately.

The Coroner was communicated with and an Inquest was held on the remains on Saturday. Dr. Walsh of Ardfinnan proved that the wounds could not be self-inflicted or the result of an accident. A verdict of wilful murder was found against some person or persons unknown.

The police searched some houses in Ardfinnan on suspicion but have obtained no clue to the murderers so far.

THE MALL

AUG 1913.

The case of Colonel Charteris-v-Dwyer Cahir for damages for trespass on ; The Mall was heard. Mr. Kenny. B.L.(instructed by Mr.O' Farrell) and Mr.Kenehan,B.L. (instructed by Mr.J.G. Skinner) for the defence.

The question at issue was the right of tying of a donkey and cart inside the railings at the entrance to the Mall. It was admitted by the plaintiff that there was a public right of way over the Mall for pedestrians, and that the defendant and other tenants on plaintiff's estate had the right to bring cars into their premises by the Mall.

The defence challenged the plaintiffs right and alleged that he had acquired a prescriptive right to do what was done, if he had no right under the lease. A lot of documentary evidence was produced to show the plaintiffs title, starting with a map of the estate dating from 1814. A conveyance of the estate which was originally owned by the Earl of Cahir, to the Charteris family dated 1853 was produced but it did not seem clear that the exact little spot, on which the trespass was complained of, was conveyed by this deed.

Evidence was given on behalf of the plaintiff that the spot, the part of the Mall immediately at the entrance, was always cared for and looked after by the state. The legal point was raised that the Mall being a public right of way, could the plaintiff acquire a perspective right as against the public. After a long hearing and legal argument the case was adjourned to the next session.

PETTY SESSIONS COURTS

CAHIR 1901

James Lynch, Thomas Lynch, John Macksey, Michael Ryan and John Ryan, were charged at the suit of Lady Beatrice Pole-Carew, and Lady Constance Butler through their solicitors Mr, G Sargint. Cahir. With having trespassed in pursuit of game on the complainants lands at Ballydrehid. Thomas Kavanagh, Keeper proved that he saw the defendants hunting game on the date reported. The defendants denied that they were hunting for game.

The Magistrate fined each of the defendants 10s costs, except James Lynch who was a mere youth, whom he fined 2s-6p and costs.

CLUTTERBUCK OF ARDFINNAN

In 1667 an estate of 2,969 acres was granted to Richard Clutterbuck in the Barony of Middlethird, Co, Tipperary. The Clutterbuck family held land in the Cahir area locality of county Tipperary from at least the mid 18th century, as there is a reference to a lease of lands from William Austin to Thomas Clutterbuck in April 1748. Richard Clutterbuck of Bannoxtown, Co. Tipperary made his will in 1825 and left his land to Thomas Clutterbuck of Kilgrogy in payment for a debt. In the mid 19th century Lorenzo Clutterbuck held estates in the parish of Ballybacon and Cahir amounting 977 acres. This land went up for sale in 1870. It is my understanding that the Clutterbuck name no longer exists in Ardfinnan

BAD WORK IN CAHIR 1926

Patrick McGrath, a farmer's son of Killeen, Butler was driving a donkey and cart home from Cahir, when he was held up by two armed and masked men, a short distance from the town, on the Ardfinnan road. They forced at the point of a revolver to dismount and hand over £12 which he had received at the bank.

OUTRAGE

Fiendish outrage in Cahir ... .On Wednesday it was reported to the police at Cahir that a donkey, the property of a poor old widow named Gorman. Who resided in Market Street had been stabbed by some party, during the previous night in a most horrible manner. District Inspector Shoveller, accompanied by Sergeant Strickland and Constable Toolari, visited the place. It was found that the shed in which the donkey was kept had been broken into and there was a gash behind the animal's ears which almost severed the head from the body.

NATIONALIST 1930

For sale a Buck Deer, over 2 years old; fit to hunt coming season, also a young Fawn Doe 3 months old.

White ferrets, ready for work. Parents direct from Scotland, 10 shillings.

Sixteen pounds of New Feathers for sale, Hunter, Lisava, Cahir.

SHANBALLY CASTLE

In March 1960, The Irish Land Commission completed the destruction, by controlled explosion, of Shanbally Castle, in Clogheen,-the largest of renowned architect John Nash's Irish Castles and once the country seat of the O'Callaghan family. C

1810. Then passing to Pole Carew and Butlers on the death of George O' Callaghan, in 1898, the impressive castle and its demesne was acquired by the Land Commission in the 50s. Whereupon having failed to find a buyer and despite local and national opposition, it was earmarked for destruction beginning in 1957. With it would be lost the vast collection of records housed there, Which tracked the history of an estate which spread at one time over 42,000 acres, from Tipperary to Cork and Limerick, some blown up with the castle's remnants and the rest consigned to a local waste paper factory. However, in a remarkable act of rescue, local historian Timmy Looney of Cahir, managed to salvage two trunks of manuscript material . and in doing so preserved for posterity an invaluable glimpse into the history and workings of the estates and tenantry of one the leading landowning families in Tipperary, of the last two centuries. It is due to this admirable act of preservation that Timmy Looney's papers, donated by his children to the Special Collections and Archives Department, Glucksman Department, University of Limerick in 2013 and recently catalogued and made available for research there.

To the rear of the remains of the Castle in the valley between the Castle and Forestry is St, Malachy's Holy Well that was frequently visited by two of the Ladies from the Castle. Before the Land Commission came to own the land, there was an annual Mass and all of the locality used to attend. John Touhy told me that the faithful used to arrive in pony and traps and there were so many that the road was blocked all the way to Shanrahan Cross. St Malachys is unique as it is covered like a roof of Yew trees and on the wettest day you won't get wet. Should you wish to see it on video type in Malachy's under Holy Wells, on Youtube.

GALTEE CASTLE

The Land Commission are to the fore again in destroying another most unique building. Galtee Castle was a mansion that was set in the most glorious site in Ireland, it was in the foothills of the Galtee Mountains at Skeheenarinkey, 10 miles from Cahir. Its original use was as a hunting lodge. It was built by the Kingston family in 1780, the third Earl Kingston remodelled it in 1825.

In the 1850s, the Kingston's were forced to sell off vast amounts of landed estate due to being in debt. This included the Lodge and up to 20,000 acres that surrounded it. There was a new estate formed and the majority of which was leased to tenant farmers.

The new owner in 1892 was called Abel Buckley who inherited the estate from his brother Nathaniel, he had previously bought sole ownership in 1873.

In the 1930s the Land Commission, who were a government agency, acquired the estate; they allocated the land between afforestation and farmers; the house was offered for sale. Again the Land Commission accepted a measly offer from a Fr. Tobin of Glanworth, Co.Cork, who wanted to use the stone and slates to build a new church in his parish. The building was torn down and dismantled in 1941.

Today there is very little left of the original building, the foundations are all that remain, nearby are some estate cottages and two gate houses. The woods and trails around the site have been turned into a public amenity known as Galtee Castle Woods.

PLOUGHING MATCH IN BARNORA 1850

The result of the ploughing at Barnora was attended by the Earl of Glengall and judged by Wm. Fennell Esq and Nicholas Doughtery Esq. In first place was Edmond Lathrigan. entitled to £5..and in second place Laurence Donnelly. entitled to £3 and in third place was John Casheen entitled to £1. A large party of the Farming Society dined at the Cahir Inn that evening.

SUNDERLANDS PUB

At the corner of Blind Street and the Cork road this was one of the busier bars in town. Tom Sunderland was a Wexford man and his wife was a Nugent from Newcastle, they had a misfortune that I covered earlier.

Tom was an electrician and when the filling station craze began, Tom had a contract with Esso and travelled around Ireland in a converted ambulance. The pub was owned by a succession of people notably the Silver Fox as he was known. While it was in the Fox's possession the building caught fire and burned to the ground. It was rebuilt by the new owner and named quite suitably The Phoenix. It is not a public house any more which is a great pity.

WELCOME INN

Without a doubt the most popular pub in the town and run by the most popular family. Oh Aye says Phil. The bar and lounge was directly across the road from the Funeral home on Blind Street. Phil Boyle was from Donegal and at first ran a bar only. He was probably the first in town to have a Chip Shop on Blind Street. The Chipper burned down and was never reopened, instead Phil opened a singing lounge as they were called. The Arcadia Dance Hall was in full flow and he was ensured a large crowd every time. Some of the Groups and Bands have Phil to thank for the start. Like all publicans at that time Phil bought a small farm and diverted his attention to farming. The downturn in the pub scene was the result you see now…houses built on the site.

IRWINS BAR

At one time it was a bar and grocery and hardware store and in my day was run by Chicken Irwin so called because of his pigeons. Then Sean took over and renovated the premises into a bar and lounge. Every character in the south gathered there. The Guinness was never put through a cooler as there was a cold room. A great topic of conversation for years was the game of cards that almost took place, I will explain later. Sean always closed on his half day every Thursday.

THE GAME OF CARDS AT IRWINS

This game went down in Irwins history and was told over and over again. This would be hard to explain to someone that is not Irish. Because the game for a start is 25 and you have to be Irish to understand it.

It was a normal fair day and the protagonists had been drinking and the conversation was running out. These were the days when money was as scarce as hen's teeth and some of the men had been at the mart so some had money and others had none or very little.

A game of cards was suggested by one of the group and at first Sean Irwin thought it was a bad idea, but decided to keep his council.

Eventually there were six seated around the table off to the side of the bar. The line up was, as Sean said …if you searched the country for six that should not be seated with each other you would fail.

Casting out for partners was John McEniry from the Clonmel road six feet of hot blood. With his back to the bar was Chess Buckley, not known for his patience and opposite him was Willie Darcy who was always cribbing, beside him was Tommy [the puck] Farrell, self explanatory. And Jack Whelan, known as black Bart and finally Jack Heffernan who had a short arm and an even shorter temper when it came to cards.

The cards were dealt and Chess had six cards so a redeal was called amid insults like he can't even deal, how do you expect him to play. Tommy Farrell told Jack Heffernan to shut up. Heffernan issued a warning to Farrell. A few threats were made and the deal resumed. A check was made this time and they all had five, the trump card was turned and it was an Ace. Willie Darcy said ..you pulled that from the bottom.....the table was thrown in the air and McEniry caught Darcy by the throat. Farrell punched Heffernan, Jack Whelan tried to run but ended up under the table. It was a half hour before order was restored and two men barred from the bar. What makes this day a bit unusual was that none of the card players was under 70. The amount they were playing for was 20c in today's money. After a few days the pair that were barred were back begging for forgiveness.

MITCHELSTOWN CAVES

Cahir is the most convenient point from which to visit the Caves of Templetenny also called Mitchelstown Caves. They lie to the south west of the town, at a distance of 15 kilometres. The caves were discovered in 1883 when men were blasting for a limestone quarry.

The entrance is 50 feet in length. At the end of this is a drop of 20 feet to a second passage, which is about 100 feet long and ending in a large chamber 80 feet in diameter and about 30 feet high. There are many other passages leading from here. There are other rooms or chambers of different sizes, each one having its own characteristics. It is reckoned that the length is about 800 feet and 570 feet wide. Stalactites and Stalagmites are in abundance as well as weeping towers and crystallizations varied in shape and form. There has been talk of more caverns attached to these caves being discovered.

CHARGE OF THE LIGHT BRIGADE

One of the greatest British military bungles and disasters in the annals of war. The British act as this was a victory in fact it was stupidity and ignorance that caused so many to die. Cardigan and Lucan were brothers in law and hated each other. Captain Louis Nolan was instructed by mouth and his orders were to attack immediately. When asked by Lucan ; where are the guns ? With a sweep of his hand Nolan said there are your guns. Looking for someone to blame the British hero blamed Nolan, which was handy because Nolan was the first to be killed.

This all took place in Balaclava on 25th October 1854. The Russians were at the far end of the valley with cannon guns that were captured from the Turks. The British commander Raglan sent men with sabres and lances down the valley to combat cannon guns.

The result was 110 killed and 161 wounded in about five minutes.

The ill fated Light Brigade returned to Cahir Army Barracks and brought with them Crimea Bob and Donkey, two war horses that survived the Charge.

PARSONS GREEN

A success story for Clogheen, the Caravan and Camping and Museums park opened for business in 1992. The large site consists of 43 acres and was purchased in 1991 by PJ Noonan, a local builder.

The venture had a lot going for it from the start. There are four natural springs forming a small river as clear as crystal. Beside one of the springs is an ancient sweat house or sauna, many centuries old. The little building is in perfect condition and is well worth a visit. The crystal waters are used for boating in small boats, supplied by the campsite. At one time there was a large country house alas it no longer exists but the stables are still there full of antiquities, like a blacksmiths forge and beside the stables are huge barns full of vintage or antique farm implements. There are permanent cabins and lots of space for caravans and motorhomes and of course tenting. The facility caters very much for families and has both indoor and outdoor playgrounds There is a beautiful leisure walk around the park, On the way you can see lots of different species of birds and different animals in the open like Alpacas and Llamas as well as different breeds of Goats, when you get back to the yard you can go for a horse drawn amble before going to the coffee and tea rooms, there is also a chip shop on site. The park is only 5 minutes walk from the Town centre. In 1833 the Green was owned by a local Magistrate and gentleman farmer called Edwin Taylor, one of the cases that he dealt with or presided over was a murder of a local woman called Mary Gorman, evidently killed by her employer, a shop owner called Mr Rice. Mr Taylor recommended the death penalty.

NATIONALIST 1931

An advert from the Nationalist from Franklin's Garage Cahir. Offered three Ford Motor Cars and one Maxwell, in perfect running order, will be sold cheap.Also Motors for hire: prices moderate.

FRACAS WITH SOLDIERS - SMART SENTENCES

At the Cahir petty sessions on Thursday, September 10th 1891. Before Major Christian, Colonel Tynte RM and Mr. William Rochfort, a case of which a good deal of local interest was centred, came on for hearing. District Inspector Shoveller prosecuted James Casey, Michael Healey, T. Connors and Patrick English, all of Cahir for having assaulted Privates John Harcourt, D.Bloom, and Wilfrid Mills, 15th Hussars and with having stabbed Harcourt in the face with a knife at Cahir on the night of 22 nd September last. It will be remembered that the case had been adjourned the previous court day because Harcourt appeared with his Face all plastered, he seemed to have got a beating . The assault took place on the night of the Hussars sports and evidence to the attack was now given by Mills, Harcourt and Bloom. The defence setup was an alibi.

Several witnesses were examined to prove that the defendants were at the Post Office at the time of the assault. The witnesses however, contradicted each other. After hearing the cases fully the courts ordered that Casey be imprisoned for two months, for assaulting Harcourt and a further two months for assaulting Bloom and Mills. Healy got one month for assaulting Bloom and another for assaulting Mills. Timothy Connors was discharged, as there was not enough evidence to prosecute him,

English was sentenced to two weeks of hard labour in each case for assaulting Harcourt and Mills.

NO PUBLIC LIGHTING IN CAHIR 1891

This is another drawback that Cahir suffers from, there is no public lighting and the inhabitants have to grope through the streets on dark nights trusting their own sharp senses and the skimpy light from shop windows. Cahir is a bustling little town that does a fair amount of business. It has a goodly population, and all things considered we think that the town has a right to be relieved of its disadvantages it labours under at present. The establishment of a Town Commission would meet the difficulty and place the town on proper footing.

GAME PROSECUTION DISMISSED

According to this you needed a permit to hunt rabbits on your own land during British rule.

Inspector McGrath charged Joseph O Brien and Thomas Donoghue, both of Cahir Abbey, with being found on the public road at Ballydavid, with a quantity of rabbits in their possession. Mr. W. Frewen appeared for both defendants.

Sergeant McNicholls stated that he was on duty at Ballydavid, he was cycling when he saw two men going towards Cahir, they had 16 rabbits which O'Donoghue was carrying. There was also a young lad with them who had a net. Witness asked the defendants to account for the game, but they made no reply. Witness seized the game.

Cross examined by Mr Frewen witness said that he was going towards Cahir. It was on the railway line that he first saw the defendants, the rabbits were not concealed in any way. The defendants were sitting down resting and they did not say that it was in Mr O' Gormans of Dranganmore that they were ferreting. Witness seized the rabbits but gave them back the fixing that the rabbits were hanging on.

Mr. Frewen said that his clients were asked by Mr.O' Gorman to come out to his place and ferret the rabbits, which were a nuisance as they were destroying his crops.

Joseph O Brien , examined, stated that he lived in Cahir Abbey. He was ferreting on Mr. O Gormans land at Dranganmore from 8.30 am to 7.30 pm. On the day in question.He had permission from Mr, O' Gormans brother, who was with them some of the time. They came along the railway line and up the path to the bridge. where they sat down for about twenty minutes resting. Donoghue had the rabbits on his shoulder.

Witness produced the written permission from Mr O'Gorman the following day. In answer to the Court witness said that he was not offered payment for killing the rabbits. Mr Frewen said that the rabbits were a nuisance ... .Mr.Troy said that he did not think that there was a poaching intent ...case dismissed.

THE STATE OF THE STREETS CAHIR 1891

The streets of Cahir are simply in a shocking state, the mud is inches deep in the middle of the roadways and the side and water channels are ornamented with piles of mud, manure and dirty refuse. It is a deplorable state that the pretty little town is continually subjected to this disgraceful disfiguration. In winter and summer too the streets are nothing better than a dirty farmyard. We have repeatedly drawn attention to this matter, and it is to be hoped for the sake of the public health of the district as well as for other considerations that some improvements will soon be made and that this eyesore will be removed once and forever. An open letter to the owners of the town......The Charteris estate.

ASSAULT ON ABBEY STREET 1891

Mary Lonergan, Cahir Abbey summoned Thomas Shea and Johanna Sullivan for assaulting her on the 24th December.

Complainant said that she was going for a bucket of water when she saw Mrs. Slattery hammering a neighbours door with a stone; Shea stopped witness, and both defendants beat her; Shea struck her with a stone in the eye and she was not able to go to Mass on Christmas day, She had to go to the doctor.

Michael Harris deposedly saw defendants strike the complainant.

The defence was that Mrs.Lonergan came out to fight and that she abused the defendants who acted in self defence.

Defendants were fined 5 shillings each.

Sheehy's Pub Ballylooby

The case by Mr Shoveller,D.I. against William Sheehy Ballylooby under the Licence Act was adjourned for the attendance of Mr.D.J.Higgins for the defendant at the next Court Session.

OBTAINING MONEY UNDER FALSE PRETENCES CAHIR 1912

Two poorly-clad labouring men named Edmond English and Michael Prendergast both of Cahir, were brought before the magistrates by District Inspector Shoveller, charged with having : unlawfully and by false pretences and with intent to defraud, obtained money from W.J, Pepper, Michael O Gorman, R,E,Smith and others at Cahir on the 11th August. The case was partly heard on the last court day when it was adjourned for more evidence. It will be remembered that the defendants represented that they were collecting money to defray the funeral expenses of an old woman, who it turned out was not dead at all.

Defendants who were not professionally represented, now pleaded guilty. Prendergast said that they had been informed that the old woman had died and they got money from Cross and some others.

They then learned that she was not dead at all and they were going to return the money. District Inspector Shoveller withdrew the other charges when the defendants pleaded guilty to one. The prisoners were sent to Gaol for 14 days with hard labour. In the evening the prisoners who had been sentenced were removed to Clonmel Gaol with a heavy escort.

FOR CRYING OUT LOUD

Tommy Purtill came from county Limerick to work for farmers and ended up working for the cattle mart for many years. A very popular man with all who knew him, Time rolled on and Tommy's health was failing. A report circulated that Tommy had passed on.Frankie Mullins heard this and immediately had a collection in the Abbey Tavern in Tommy's memory. They collected a substantial sum, THE PUB PATRONS WERE EVEN GOING TO GIVE THEIR LATE FRIEND A GUARD OF HONOUR and that evening Tommy arrived into the pub for a drink. They presented Tommy with the money to have a drink and poor old Tommy enjoyed the story and the pints.

CAHIR IN THE 60S

Every town that you passed through in the 60s you would always see children playing on the street and helping out in the fields, we were all open air reared and no one wanted to be inside. My mother used to send me to Doon county Limerick for all of the summer school holidays , from when I was about 6 or 7 years. I was sent to the Cross of Cloggan on the bus with a label tied to my collar. All those summers were spent working in the fields at hay or in the bog bringing in the turf with an ass and cart. My aunt had seven children of her own and the company was brilliant. She had an open fire fuelled by turf and the cooking and baking was all done in metal pots. I never had town bread while I was there. When the holidays were over we were back to the grind, all of us hated school because of the beatings from the savage teacher. After school we could be anywhere across fields, down the park, up the mountain the parents had nothing to worry about. The world was a safer place for children and we were easily amused. The railway embankment was just made for sliding down all day on cardboard boxes, we made our own fishing rods and went to Jacksons stream to catch brickeens, the town dump was at the rear of Barry's garage and we would spend days down there without catching any disease. If you had any money which was as scarce as anything, you could go to Jackie Nolans to listen to the jukebox. Sunday was the matinee at the cinema and that was the greatest thrill of all, especially if it was a cowboy film. Every year Tom Duffy's Circus would arrive to Loobys field. I cannot express the excitement. You might get a few pence from a farmer that was hunting cattle or sheep through the streets and country. All the sweets used to be a penny, gobstoppers, blackjacks, macaroons and bulls eyes. Every Christmas the boys got a gun and holster and the girls got a doll. Down the well field with our new weapons all 60 or 70 of us. Behind Aldi there used to be a pond that freezes over every winter and we all skated on it. School dragged on and on and when it was time to be released another kind of life awaited.

AFTER SCHOOL

While I was going to school, it could be called work. I used to bring the previous night's films to the railway station in their heavy boxes. This was done before school and I daren't be late. After school I would collect that night's films and wheel them on a handcart to the cinema. This was a tough job for an 11 year old. I did this work as well as working in the projection box at night. The manager was Brendan Mulcair who later went to Carrick on Suir. The boxes of film always came from Thurles and were always sent on to Fethard, it was the Capitol group of cinemas.

My mother Bridie Lonergan and Phil Buckley worked as the ticket ladies.

By now I am 14 years and England beckons so I went to Wolverhampton and moved in with the Cronins from Bengurrah. When you leave school all your friends disperse, some die, some go away and never return. Some you look up when you hit England. I used to call to Folkestone to see Noel Haide who lived in Love Lane, aptly named. I soon got tired of England and returned after a short while. The Factory was the next stop for a while. Following a myriad of jobs, I worked at a system built housing firm. with Cannon Jimmy English and Patsy Frazer and Johnny Lonergan. I never finished an apprenticeship, a few weeks in the mental home, lots of jobs that I hated and then a woman came along. The first marriage did not last. Daughter Cher was born in England my son Lee was born in Tipperary. On my own again for a few years. I Had a go at the Stained Glass trade and survived for a while but the PVC windows put an end to that. Worked for years with Mickey Mac and Tommy and Mickey Neill, which of these were the craziest is anyone's guess.?. I never mentioned that Pat Beary, Paudi Blyth, Davy

Lonergan and myself had a rock band in the 60s. We never played anywhere but boy did we look the part. We used to go around in a group in our hippie gear and Bearys DKW van. We went to see Thin LIzzie at the City Hall in Cork and because of the way that we were dressed the cork gurriers set about us and gave us the mother and father of all beatings. We looked so bad that Captain Beary wanted to come the next time.

SETTLING DOWN

Like most guys my age, drinking played a big part in all the trouble but it is difficult to give up. Out of the blue another woman entered my life and there was no escape from Margaret Slattery. We Had a magical few years living it up, dances, holidays and then the bomb dropped ... .I have news for you.....meant only one thing: another baby on the way, Waylon Bartholomew arrived on the scene followed after a few years by Emmet Martin. I thought that would be it ...but no..14 years later Ruth Bridget arrived and that was that. Being a law abiding human being I built a house in Garryroan, without planning permission, this caused a lot of problems. It was time to call Michael Ferris the Tipperary TD. Deputy Ferris sorted the problem but at a cost. I had to join the Labour Party and it was the best thing that I ever did. I ran for election three times and got elected twice. The first Labour Councillor in Cahir for 44 years. Along the line I joined the A.A. and thanks to the membership and Jerry from Ardfinnan I was successful. I pulled myself together with the help of my Margaret and life has been good to both of us. That is apart from Mag's cancer and bad heart and my dodgy heart and kidneys and diabetes, we both play the cards that we are dealt.

A few tragedies along the way my sister Mary suffered the loss of two of her daughters, Roma was murdered in Holland which is enough to destroy anyone and then Avril who was involved in drugs and there was no talking to her. Her remaining daughter Sophia was left to hold things together in Holland. Bridie my mother died and left a hole in all of our lives. I think my mother can be proud of us all. Bobby in Kerry and Mary and myself, we all turned out alright.

Bridie Lonergan had a nephew in Kenya in Kitui for over 60 years. He was responsible for building several schools and his crowning glory was a University in Nairobi. Tony Woods was his name; he died in 2023 and was buried in Kenya, the papers said of him ... .The man with the big heart breathes his last…

PEOPLE AND THEIR SAYINGS

Timmy Fitzgerald Loughloher

If I was any happier it would be wasted.

Jerry Sheehan Church Street.

You know what I mean kinda we'll say.

Michael Kennedy Cahir Abbey Upper

That was alright anyway.

Tommy Meehan

My lovely Kathleen

Fintan Moore

Nil aon Fintan mar do Fintan fein

Johnny Regan

In former times after that.

Frank Mullins

If it was raining soup I'd have a fork.

Archie Condon, closing the bar for the night

All ashore that's going ashore.

Phil Boyle The welcome inn

Oh aye.

Peter Riordan, Barrack Street

I was dreaming about you last night.

Tom Donoghue, Mountain View Drive

Dingle Dongle.

Lawrie Williamson

The last of the underarm bowlers.

Paddy English,Garryroan

He's a friendly old freezer.

Jim Costigan Castlecoyne.

Sandy…He called everyone Sandy because he was bad with names.

KIT CONWAY

He was born near Burncourt Cahir on Dec. 3rd 1899 and was reared in Clogheen workhouse, on leaving the workhouse he went to work for a farmer in Coolagarranroe near Burncourt, called William English, he was paid 2 shillings a week. He was known in those days as Christy.

Kit, as he later became known, joined the British army in 1915. He was well versed in Irish history and did not believe that England was fighting for small nations. He was discharged from the forces and returned to Ireland. In 1919 he joined the 6th Battalion, Skeheenarinky, 3rd Tipperary Brigade. He was appointed drill sergeant in the Burncourt Company where he was noticed by Dan Breen and Sean Treacy and he was recruited into Sean Hogan's Flying Column in 1920. Right from the start he was seen to be brave. In an attack on Ballyporeen R.I.C barracks he was plainly exposed to enemy fire. The attack on the barracks was successful due to Conway's daring. The column was pursued by mounted lancers near Ballygiblin and managed to lead the enemy to a bog and there the lancers were at a disadvantage, the column made their escape. At the outbreak of the Civil War he went with his republican friends, he joined the anti Treatyites and fought to the end of the Civil War. As a convinced socialist he campaigned for the workers and underprivileged. Kit made his way to Spain to fight fascism and with 229 fellow socialist republicans was in Cordoba defending the Spanish Republic, He died in the Jarama Valley while leading his men into battle on February 12 th 1937. In that action 19 Irishmen died that day. A plaque in Irish, English and Spanish stands at the entrance to Burncourt village in memory of Kit Conway.

KENDRICKS PUB

John Kendrick and his wife Bridie owned a public house in Abbey Street called the Abbey Tavern. John was tired of the pub landlord's life, one night the topic was new films and John was asked; did you see The Planet of the Apes; every bloody day was the reply.

LADY'S ABBEY ARDFINNAN

A Lady lived in France by the name of Sarah Maguire, at this time there were a lot of Irish names in France, because it was in preference to England. This woman had a dream about this Abbey, in her dream she learned that being buried in this holy ground, purgatory would be dispensed with. She decided to come to Ireland and search for the blessed place. She spent most of the year visiting all the Abbeys and Monasteries all around the country. When she finally reached Ardfinnan she recognised the Abbey from her dream.

She went back to France and willed to be buried at the Abbey. When she finally passed away, to fulfil her wish, Her body had to be put in a barrel of brandy to preserve it for the journey. Her grave is in the corner of the old monastery, her tombstone with her name and age are still readable.

Some people used to believe the Monastery was called after this lady.

This is not true, experts say it was a Carmelite Abbey and is called after Our Lady.

THE DOLE LADY

The Social Welfare office, if I may call it that, was a private house in Market Street. This was in the 70s and was lorded over by a spinster called Alice Smith. There may have been rule books about dealing with people's claims, but Alice never bothered with such trivia. First of all you had to call her Miss Smith or there would be no transaction. She was about 4 ft 9 inches tall and the terror of her domain. It was entirely up to her whether you got your payment or not. There were no appeals in her book. Market Street is a secluded quiet street of residents that have lived in harmony forever. She lived till 102 ……on her 100th birthday the street geared up for a street party, but Alice wanted to send invitations to those that she wanted to attend, not everybody you understand. John Keith personally delivered a letter explaining why he would NOT turn up.

The rest of the residents were not so brave and most of them seemed to have someplace to go urgently. Although she got a huge crowd at her funeral.

A. A. MEETINGS

When I first gathered the courage to attend an A.A. meeting it was in Ardfinnan and an empty room, except for one man Jerry. The two of us sat for almost a year before the meeting attracted other members. Before very long we had about a dozen regular and a few irregular males and females. Jerry was my sponsor and I am forever thankful to him. Not all alcoholics are crazy but we had our share. One night we had a discussion and the topic was ambitions and how we wished to turn out.

M's contribution was that his ambition was to sit on the bonnet of a Jaguar, with a machine gun on his lap, a fag in his mouth and drive through the village of Ardfinnan. Another night he produced a bottle of vodka in the middle of a meeting and asked if anyone wanted a drink. Another night that I will never forget is T, a normally loud man but this night not a word did he utter. It was raining and Jerry asked if I would drive T home. We were passing the village Church when he asked me to stop the car across from the building, we waited for a while and I asked why were we stopped…..He's in there tonight he said….I asked who….My little boy he said…what's he doing I asked….He's dead, killed in a motorbike accident he said. I cannot express the feeling of sorrow for the man.

SCARAGH TO KILCOMMON

In the 1920s the Manager of Cahir Estates and the local farmers from Scaragh down across the fields to Kilcommon, with sheer tenacity brought flowing water down across the roadways and fields overland and wooden troughs. This was of benefit to all the landowners that the stream passed through. The original plan was to bring it to the estate farmyard. In some stretches it flowed in wooden troughs on top of ditches and under ditches and roads. When it came to Clonmore it divided and a spur was brought to the Parade field and it continued through O'Donnell's land onto the field beside Barrets in Kilcommon. Until this time the water had to be brought to the animals in barrels and churns. The landowners used to clean it every year. This was before the group water scheme.

CAHIR 1819

Last Sunday morning between eight and nine o 'clock two young men armed, broke in the door of Cahir Bleach, about a mile from the town, they then proceeded to ransack the house and by breaking a large chest succeeded in getting a case of horse pistols there. In another part of the house they got a blunderbuss all in excellent order. The people of the house having gone to Cahir to attend Divine Worship and the house being under no other protection than that of a young servant girl, the villains affected their escape for the present.

About the same hour the house of J, Heffernan, of Drangan seven miles distant of the Bleach Green near Kilmoyler, was entered by two men who were admitted unexpectedly, as one of the fellows on coming to the door asked to be employed in digging potatoes ; immediately after they withdrew they returned instantly, one armed with a sword and the other with a pistol. As in the previous case all the family were gone to Mass, excluding the servant maid, whom they asked for firearms.The maid said that there was none, they insisted that there were and proceeded to search the house. They broke a trunk in which they got a shot bag and a pay book containing some bank notes.They handed the pocket book to the servant girl saying ..deliver this to your master as you will be accountable for the notes…for we want nothing but arms. In another place they found a gun and some silver in a desk. They gave the silver to the maid and said ..give this to your master. They then decamped, taking with them the shot bag and gun. A worker saw them and followed them, getting assistance from Mr. Richard Butler of Ballyslateen. He and his party had to cross the river Suir after a chase of 4 miles. The pursuers were successful in capturing the culprits and brought them before Mr.Stephen O'Meagher Esq of Kilmoyler, who sent them to Cahir Bridewell. From there they were sent to Cashel. Ed.Lonergan was the nephew of the celebrated Michael Stack who was executed a few years ago.

OLD SAYINGS

The smallest thing you should put in your ear is your elbow.

They're all afraid of the calf, and none afraid of the bull.

If he had twice as many brains, he would still be a half wit.

Vote early and vote often.

All his geese are swans.

Broken Irish is better than clever English.

Never burn your lips on another man's porridge.

The old dog for the hard road.

The truth never choked a man.

You've got to do your own growing. No matter how tall your father was.

Forgetting a debt, doesn't mean it's paid.

The older the fiddle the sweeter the tune.

Fast women, slow horses never made a man.

He didn't lick it off a stone.

Never give cherries to a pig or advice to a fool.

There's many a slip between cup and lip.

CAHIR PARK AFC

The birth of Irish soccer goes back to 1878, Cahir Park AFC was founded in 1910 and it is one of the oldest in the country. The reason for it's slow start is it was played by predominantly British soldiers.Tipperary was a Catholic and Nationalist stronghold and it did not suffer change easily. Cahir was a garrison town and it took time for outsiders to get the courage to play it. In Cahir park's history even after the founding of the club they continued to play against the military. Up to this time it was always barracks against barracks.

In the 1920s the establishment of a Tipperary league with only two civilian teams, Cahir Park and Clonmel Comrades FC. Some time later the third would come along in the guise of the Tipperary Wanderers.

Wanderers and the Park were to represent Tipperary in the national leagues and cups. Soccer was not the most popular game in the country and WWI was another topic which divided peoples opinion. Again the connection between soccer as a British garrison was hard to shake off. As noted in Cahir Park's history, that up until the formation of the Irish Free State virtually all games were played against military teams.

The men who played for Cahir Park came from all walks of life. On the team that won the Tyler Cup, was a butcher, a post office clerk, a public house owner and James McNamara a well known Gaelic Footballer who won an all Ireland with Tipperary in 1920 and also played on the Tipperary team on Bloody Sunday. Despite soccer's name as a garrison game, Cahir Park was different as it was open to men from all walks of life. Cahir is not only one of Ireland's oldest clubs. It included very few soldiers and police unlike many other clubs. The GAA's ban on the game did not help or encourage the country's people to play soccer. Big towns had the ability to support more than one sport. Soccer found a home in Cahir Park, and over a hundred years later it is going strong and it paved the way for other towns.- James Deegan.

Ballylooby in the 1950s there were 5 Lafford brothers playing on the hurling team at the same time.

THE APPLE FARM

Tom Sampson moved to Canada in the middle sixties and sold his sixty acres at Moorestown to William and Ali Traas who came from the Netherlands, William came from Zeeland and Ali was from Kampen. The plan was to have a fruit farm on the land and it took some time to come to fruition. They purchased the land in 1967 and in 1968 the first orchard tree plants were planted. Meanwhile they tried growing cabbage, even tulips and all manner of agriculture crops. They had two sons Cornelius and Henry. Born in 1968 and 1971. Following a tragic motorbike accident Henry lost his life, this was a difficult time for the family. William set about building the caravan and camping park in 1980, the camping and caravan park was a success and the fruit business prospered. Cornelius set out to expand the business and began making fruit juices, as well as apples and pears the strawberries are another part of the business. Seanie Lonergan and Michael O'Neill did a lot of work on the camping facilities.

When the job finished William suggested that we seal the deal with a little drink and we went to the house for a whiskey, after a few drams we started to play a game of draughts, not a game for the tipsy. An argument broke out over the rules, it seems that the Dutch have different rules to us Irish. William produced the rule book and it happened to be in Dutch …..not a lot of good to me. Ali had to intervene and she could not believe that two grown men would act like kids. William towards the end of his life started to write poetry and he made the mistake of asking for my opinion.

WILLIE MAHER

Little Willie Maher of Kilcoran worked for Kathleen O'Brien when he retired from the County Council, I had the honour of being with him in those days. Willie was 85 and had a shake in his head and hands. One day I asked if he was ever out of the country, he said that he was in America once, I asked where…he said that he could not remember but they had very big houses. That evening I asked his daughter if it was true and she said that he was in New York with her sister…..Big Houses.

WALK TALL

Another Cahir man that made it to the top of the tree is a man called Henry Ryan, we don't know him as Ryan but he is more famous as the shoe maker to royalty. Rayne. Henry Ryan left Cahir shortly after the famine and went to England. As he got more popular the name evolved into the now famous brand Rayne, Henry's son was shoemaker to the British royals and famous stage actors. His grandson Edward was Knighted for his services to the royals..They made shoes for three successive Queens. In the epic film Cleopatra, Elizabeth Taylor wore Raynes

Shoes as well as Vivien Leigh and Diana Rigg in the Avengers. For the first time Rayne's shoes can be bought in Ireland as they opened an outlet in Grafton street in 2024. The fashion magazine also informs us that the British Queen had a staff member break in her shoes for her, as she liked her comfort.

THE WHITEHEAD BYRON

Col.John Whitehead Byron was born November, 1840. in the historic town of Cahir. The greatest part of his childhood was spent with his grandfather John Byron about 2 miles from Cahir, when he was 15 he went to New York. At the break of the rebellion, he promptly responded to Lincoln's call for troops. He joined the State Militia which became Meagher's Zouaves with its commander Thomas Francis Meagher at the helm. He fought with distinction at Blackburn's Ford and Bull Run He fought at all the main encounters and was wounded and taken prisoner. His release came when he was exchanged for another prisoner. He set sail for Ireland in an attempt to help shake off the yoke of British rule. He was arrested and sent to prison for 2 years, they wanted him to turn traitor and he refused, he was released and put on a ship that was bound for America. He therefore returned to New York and became Adjutant - General of the Fenian Brotherhood and later Inspector of that order. Col.Byron was actively prominent in the affairs of the Grand Army of the Republic.

GRAVEYARD OLD CHURCH ST

Here lyeth the body of Elizabeath Gideon who departed this life on the 7 day of February and year 1747 aged 60 years.

Erected by Edmond Purtil of Cahir as the last tribute of duty and affection to his virtuous mother, Mary Purtil alias O'Dwyer of the Ancient

Milesian stock of Cillnamanac, who departed this life invoking the assistance of the Mother of God, Dec 18th 1846 aged 88.

Catholic reader pray for her.

This headstone placed here by Mrs, Ebsworth of St.Kilda Australia in memory of her grandfather, Mr.Michael Purtil who is still living and in the 83rd year of his age,,,,and at his demise will make this his last resting place. Also his wife Catherine Purtil who died in 1885 aged 60 years. And 2 of their children who died young, and his brother Edmond Purtil who died 1887 aged 80 years....erected 1889.

Bessie Georgina De Renzy, died April 9th 1854.

Erected by the Earl of Glengall to the memory of his faithful Valet

Pierre Vial, a native of France who departed this life on the 18th November 1844 aged 52 years.

Here lie ye remains of William Prendergast of Lisava who departed this life May 16th 1739 aged 56 years.

Here lies the remains of Mr.Martin Meara of Cahir; he was a young man of bright parts and unspotted innocence who died 29th Jan. 1774 in the 24th year of his age, also the body of his sister Ellen.

Here lies ye body of Anne.who died 29th September 1767 age 7 years.

MISSING OFFICERS FATE

FAREWELL LETTER RECEIVED FROM INSPECTOR POTTER

CAHIR MYSTERY

TRAGIC SEQUEL TO RECENT AMBUSH IN CO. TIPPERARY

Mrs. Potter, wife of District-Inspector Gilbert Potter, Cahir, who has been missing since an ambush that he ran into near Clogheen about three weeks ago and who, it was reported, has been executed, received a small packet from her husband Sunday evening, containing a farewell letter, diary, signet ring and gold watch. The letter was dated April 27th and bore a Cahir postmark.

In the course of the letter he said; that he was writing it in the morning, as he would be executed that day. He bade farewell to his wife and four little children in affectionate terms.

The news caused great excitement in Cahir where it was believed that the previous letter was not from a genuine source.

Rev. H Dene, M,A, Rector at service in the Protestant Church on Sunday spoke in touching terms of Mr Potter. The Dead March was chanted.

Crowds of sympathisers of all denominations visited the bereaved family.

FORMATION OF THE CIVIC GUARD

On the seventeenth of August in 1922

Through the gates of Dublin Castle, Marched a group of men in blue.

By a brand new Irish Nation their orders were laid down.

To bring peace and law and order to valley hill and town

In those days of civil warfare they knew their task was great

Knowing that for some, even death might be their fate.

They were called the ..Civic Guard..they were young and strong and true

They knew their only weapon was the uniform of blue.

TOWNLANDS OF CAHIR

Knocknaboha.	Hill of the cows.
Reiska.	Wet place…Marshy place.
Knocka.	Hilly place.
Lisava.	Fort of the birches.
Monaraha.	Bog of the fort.
Garryclogher.	Stoney garden.
Killeenabutler.	Butler's little church.
Ratheen.	Little fort.
Clonmore.	Big meadow.
Cooleaclamper.	Corner of contention,disputed land.
Austin.	Augustinian land.
Ballylegan.	Town of the standing stone.
Loughaun.	Little lake.
Killemly.	Church of the lake /marsh.
Monaderreen.	Bog of the oak grove.
Rathmore.	Big fort.
Ballynamona.	Town of the bog.
Barnora.	Norah's Gap.
Carrigeen.	Little rock.

Edenmore.	Big ridge.
Farrannagark	Land of the hens.
Keylong.	Long narrow strip.
Killeigh.	Grey church-field church.
Knockfeagh.	Stag hill.
Cranagh.	A place full of trees.
Scart.	Cluster of bushes.

CAHIR AND DISTRICT

Ardfinnan	Ard Fionain	Fionain's heights
Ballylooby	Baile an Lubach	town on the bend of the river.
Ballyporeen	Baile an poirin	Town of the little potato
Burncourt	Court doite	the burned court.
Cahir	Cathair dun Iscaig	Town of the fort of fishes
Clogheenan	Cloice	.Little rock.
Grange	A Barn	
Goatenbridge	Gabair an droichid	
Kilmoyler	Cill Moylar	Moylar's church

New Castle   Caislan Nua

New Inn   Loch Ceann   Lough   Kent.   High
Lake.

Poulnamuck   The hole of the pigs

Skeheenarinky   The dancing bush.

Bengurragh   Blue peak   formerly a bullring.

The Osiery   Willow growing area.

The Lacka   the side of a hill.

The well field   Just off   Upper Abbey street.

Casey's field or rock field   Abbey Street.

Blind Street   Now called Lower Abbey Street.

Cowboys den   the well field.

Maddens lane   Just off   Church street.

Ramcats lane   .Just off   Pearse street.

Dillons Bohereen Just off   Cashel road.

Hospital Hill   Cork road.

The Ha Ha   Beside St.Paul's Church.

St, Patricks stone   Ardfinnan road.

Brewery lane   Just off   Upper abbey street.

SWISS COTTAGE

Built by Richard Lord Cahir in 1810. It was designed by John Nash, a well known Regency architect who designed St, Pauls Church in Cahir.

Vacant for several years, it was restored by the OPW. Built in the Cottage Orne style it has some of the first commercially produced Parisienne wallpaper. A view of the Bosporus, is the pattern by Paul Dufour. Following the restoration it was opened to the public. In times gone by it was occupied by Eugene Heaphy who made Fishing rods and tied fishing flies, said to be one of the best in the country. Rumour has it that the foxy Lord used to entertain the young girls of the town in the Cottage without the wife's knowledge, as a result there was an extraordinary amount of red haired children in Cahir and its environs.

Adjacent to the Cottage site there was an attempt to build an Abbey, a sister building of Glastonbury Abbey in 720 but it was never built even though it is said that the foundations were put in.

HAN MADDEN

Now known as Maddens Lane it was once the home of Han Madden and her family. She had a very small house from which she ran a business. She had a huge rock in her kitchen on which she prepared tripe for boiling. Han also made black and white puddings and as everyone knows puddings are made from pigs blood, so the smell had to be hard to bear.

Tripe is made from animal stomachs mostly from sheep and pigs and has to be boiled for hours and hours. Hard work did not bother Han. Another string to her bow was that she used to skin pigs and boil the pelt for more food. The butchers in town supplied her with the offal.

Times were hard in the late 1890s and many were glad of Han's offal; the tripe was at the very low cost of food and many would not eat it.

Health and safety did not exist in those days and still there are no recorded deaths from food poisoning. Han lived a long life despite the conditions of her lodgings and workplace

ST MARY'S CHURCH.

Built in 1833 by Fr.Michael Tobin. 50 years later it had to be repaired by Rev.Maurice Mooney P.P. An older church than the present one had been erected on the spot in 1791. Prior to this the parishioners worshipped in a thatched chapel that stood near the entrance to Cahir Park. This was a chapel of the Penal Days and the Butlers of that period were Catholics and provided the people of Cahir with a place of worship.

In 1895 Charteris leased almost an acre of land to the Church.

The Rev William O Donnell who was here between 1924 and 1933 got a further extension. He also purchased the present Parochial House and in 1904 the Curate had the Curates House built and called it St.Maryville.

Seanie Lonergan

CAHIR CASTLE
BY JOHN MACKEY

By Suir's flowing water
The scene of ancient slaughter
Stands the Castle in its glory
Looking down on all the town
The Castle never changes
And the people are not lasting
So it knows the people's story
And it tells it to the river

Does it mention to the river
The pain of all the ages
And the worries of the people
Which their hearts did burden down
For it saw the face of Cromwell
And the hunger of the famine
And the war that raged around it
As the Harp replaced the Crown.

It saw the youth of Ireland
Set out for Europe's mainland
To defend the oppressed peoples
In those tragic World Wars.
But very few returned
To the Suirs lovely valley
And the Cross below the Castle
Tells their names for evermore.

Is the story that the Castle
Tells the river in the moonlight
All about the little children
That round its walls have fun
Does it say though now they're happy
But like children of past ages
They shall see their share of sorrow
Ere their life on earth is run.

For the Castle knows from history
That life is but a shadow
And that people are but glimpses
Of pilgrims passing through
It has seen the rich and famous
Pass away and be forgotten
Like leaves upon the Autumn trees
When winter breezes blew.

But the story that the Castle
Tells the river in the moonlight
Is a story that has never reached
The ear of mortal man
Still the river keeps on singing
As It flows towards the ocean
And the Castle in the moonlight
It will never see again.

A DIFFERENT LOOK AT D.I POTTER

On Bloody Sunday, November 1920. A heavily armed party of RIC and Black and Tans and Auxiliaries forced its way into Croke Park during a Gaelic football match between Dublin and Tipperary and indiscriminately murdered by shooting 14 people and wounding 80 of which 16 died later of their wounds. This was in reprisal for the IRA killing of 14 British intelligence officers known as the Cairo Gang. They were a handpicked squad that was assembled for the purpose of destroying the IRA.

Indiscriminate reprisals had become British policy from 1919 onwards and it is within this framework that the following two incidents ensued.

The following was given by P Mahon about his father, an RIC man.

One night D.I. Potter called my father into his office, handed him a list containing 16 names of local men and told him to take a party of Black and Tans to their homes and shoot them. He said that they were IRA suspects. My father was shocked and challenged the order saying:

I have not joined the Police Force to become a murderer and I therefore refuse to carry out the order, after some discussion Potter withdrew it.

The next night was a repeat of the first order but in the presence of others, including Black and Tans and this time it was reinforced by Potter drawing his revolver, placing it on the desk, and saying that if anyone objected they would have the contents of the revolver. My father again refused and Potter again backed down after some discussion.

The next day my father was instructed to take a squad of 10 Black and Tans out on patrol by bike. He was convinced that this was his execution party but to his surprise the patrol went off without incident. In a garrison town of course some people will hold the British in high esteem, after reading this account I do not think that Potter deserves the veneration afforded him by some people.

BRIDIE LADRIGAN

When We Lived in Abbey Street, Ladrigans was our grocery shop and like everyone at that time we had a book for credit that was paid for every week. We knew that the Ladrigans were involved in the Civil war and the war of Independence but never guessed how brave Bridie was.

Bridie, as my memory of her, was a quiet and refined woman.

Her brothers were in the IRA, Mikey was most prominent and Bridie was in Cumann Na Mban as was Molly Harrigan of the Mountain Road .

Ladrigans was searched regularly by the British, one night Neddy her brother had a narrow escape, as they broke in the front door, Neddy climbed the back wall and onto the railway and hid behind the pillars on the railway bridge.

At an IRA meeting in Tincurry HQ attended by locals and Bridie who was head of Cahir Cumann Na Mban, was asked to collect money for the brigade but she defied them and refused on the grounds that the Cumann only collected for food parcels for IRA prisoners in various camps and prisons, and not for active free members. Bridie was not supposed to wear the Green Cumann uniform but did wear it, It was confiscated by Potter on several occasions. On fair days the Cumann collected for prisoners despite opposition from the P.P. the RIC and the Military. During the Civil

War Timmy Looney's father drove Bridie and other Cumann members to Clonmel on his sidecar to collect first aid supplies for the Tincurry and local IRA brigades, which was a major crime at the time, as the Free Staters were on the verge of taking Clonmel at the time. Bridie and Timmy Looney drove the sidecar back from Clonmel in full view of the Free State soldiers. The British used to purposely put up posters in shop windows advertising for recruits in the British army. As they entered Bridie's shop with their poster she took it down straight away and was told by a soldier to put it back. Bridie defiantly said that you get paid to do your dirty work and slammed the door. As far as I know none of the Ladrigans married and they worked in the shop all their lives.

THE VICTORIA CROSS

Michael Murphy was born in Cahir, Co.Tipperary. Murphy was born on the 5th September 1831. The records in the church show that he was baptised on the same day. His parents were John Murphy and Hanora Sheehan. According to the marriage register, Michael Murphy married on the 26th February 1854. His wife was called Mary Walsh and the two witnesses were, Patrick Walsh and Hanna Prendergast.

He joined the 17th Lancers in 1855 as a farrier. His first outing with the Lancers was to march from Cahir to Dublin. In 1857 war broke out in China and the battalion set off for Woolwich where they would board a ship for the Orient. After moving all over the Orient he was engaged in fighting in India at Lucknow where he fought gallantly. He played no small part in the relief of Azimghur and in operations in the Shanabar region. When the battalion was in pursuit of the rebels near Nathupur, it was here that he won his Victoria Cross.

For daring and gallantry on 15 April 1858, when engaged in pursuit of Koer Singh's army from Azimghur, in having rescued Lieutenant Hamilton, Adjutant of the 3rd Sikh Cavalry, who was wounded and surrounded by the enemy. Farrier Murphy cut down several men, and although himself severely wounded, he never left Lieutenant Hamilton's side until support arrived.

He was discharged from the Lancers as being unfit to serve, and he returned to civvy street and the North of England, he settled in Darlington. During this time there was an accusation of Murphy and some stolen hay and because of this the British establishment looked for the return of his Victoria Cross, The British wanted him to forfeit the award and it is now in Durham Museum. Michael died in Darlington in 1893, During the court hearing Michael wore the Victoria Cross every day. When he died, his will said that he left everything to his second wife Elizabeth the sum and full effects of £21.

THE LADY RETURNS TO LIFE

This story was told by Mr Dan O Donnell ,Garryroan,.age 68…in 1988.

A wealthy English family came to Ireland and purchased a large tract of land just outside of Cahir.

The story goes that there were four daughters and one son in the family.

The girls were very handsome and were much admired especially in the hunting field, all being great horsewomen.

Isobel the youngest was considered the …the flower of the flock…and was engaged to a wealthy English Earl, She was taken suddenly ill and was attended by two doctors. She died within a week and was buried in the family vault in Tubrid. That night the three sisters stayed up longer than usual, the father and mother and the servants having retired sometime earlier.

Suddenly there was a knock on the hall door and the eldest sister remarked…if Isobel were not dead I would swear that it was her knock, at the same time going to the front door to see who the late caller was.

Imagine her surprise when she opened the door and found Isobel standing dressed exactly as she had been laid out in the coffin. The sister gave a loud scream and the other sisters rushed to the door at once and with great presence of mind took charge of Isobel and put her straight to bed.

Some of the servants who arrived at the scene attended the eldest sister who had fainted. The doctor who arrived very soon afterwards and having done all that was necessarily for Isobel, he and all the members of her family listened to her strange story as told by herself.

I awoke from a beautiful sleep in a small dark room, lighted by a lantern and a man standing by, whom I recognised as our old butler. He had a hold of my hand and I felt a stinging pain in one of my fingers. I must have shouted at him, as he let go of my hand and ran away leaving the lantern behind. I sat up and got out of my narrow bed, taking the lantern with me and made for the door. When outside I found that I was in Tubrid churchyard beside the family vault.

I scrambled across the wall and got to the road and ran home as fast as I could. A few days later the butler was located and confessed to his crime. I stole the key to the vault because I knew that Isobel was buried with valuable rings on her fingers and jewellery. Having failed to remove them from the finger joints she screamed and I ran in terror.

The doctor explained that Isobel was not dead but only in a trance and that the cut on the finger joint put the blood circulating through the body and was the means of saving her life.

She fully recovered and she married the English Earl and had a family.

Dan said that he tells the tale as told to him.

ANOTHER GHOST STORY

Told by John Tierney, Chamberlainstown New Inn.

There was once a man searching for a proper sponsor for his child in Baptism. He was very hard to please and no person in his parish was good enough to stand for his child. He went off in search of a sponsor and on the road he met Almighty God and asked Him would he stand for his child. The Almighty answered no, because he said that you are not the same as any man in this world. The man went on and met the Devil the Devil asked him would he do to stand for the child and the man said no, because he was evil. He went on again and he met Death and death said he would stand for the child because he was the same to all men. He brought Death home with him to stand for the child.

The child grew up to be a man and death because he was his godfather gave him a special gift. The gift was that the man would know if any sick person would die. Always when he called to see a sick person if Death was at the foot of the bed he knew that the person would die. The people had great faith in this young man and he used to make great sums of money by making up useless medicines and giving it to the sick people when he saw Death standing at the head of the bed. One day the young man went to a house and found the people crying, because their brother was dying.

Death was standing at the foot of the bed and he knelt and said a prayer and then thought of a plan, he told the people to turn the bed around and then Death would be at the head of the bed and that the person would live. Death was very angry and told the young man that the next time that he went on his knees that he would take him. The man said that it would be a long time.

The young man went around curing people and any time that Death was at the foot of the bed, he had it turned around.

One day the man went to a friend's wake and the relatives were saying the Rosary so he knelt down. Death appeared and said that he had trapped him…The young man died shortly afterwards.

MCCRAITH AND MCGRATH

Laura McCraith was from Loughloher and was a writer and painter. She wrote one book that was highly acclaimed called The Suir From its source to the sea. The photography was done by P.J.Condon of Church Street Cahir. This was published in 1912 and she also wrote another book called A Green Tree.

There is a large cluster of McGraths in Tubrid, located a short distance from Cahir. They are descended from a clan which had migrated from the southern part of Clare to the Cahir area in the 1500s where they started a bardic school. The family was on the same school level as the Keatings.

The McCraiths of Tubrid were Catholics and if they were connected to the Loughloher McCraiths then it would be expected that they were also Catholic. This would have presented a problem in the Penal times 1700s when Catholics were not allowed to own land as well as a long list of other things that were forbidden. In later years it was shown in the census of 1901 that the Loughloher McCraiths belonged to the Church of Ireland in other words Protestants. This would explain the family's ability to retain their land through the Penal Times.

LONERGANS - HOW TO TELL THEM APART.

The name is prolific in Tipperary and as a way of telling them apart is the nickname, some complementary and some not.

Lonergans the pound	On the Clonmel road
The Boxer Lonergans	The Jobber Lonergans.
The Sniper Lonergans	The Robber Lonergans
The Ring Lonergans	The Buckley Lonergans.
The Patsy Phil Lonergans	The Richie Ned Lonergans

The German Jim Lonergans	The Brien Lonergans.
The Yank Lonergans	Johnny Lonergan the Cyclist .
The Gag Lonergans	The Jimmy Oliver Lonergans
The Badger Lonergans	Peg Leg Lonergans.
The Run Buddy's Lonergans	Lonergans the Mountain.
The Favourite Lonergans	Mick Kojack Lonergan.

The Archbishop of Cashel Donat O Lonergan founded the Cashel Corporation in the year 1216

Mick Kojack Lonergan returned from America and initially bought a pub in Golden, he built a house around Poulnamuck and kept a few greyhounds. He had a pair of dogs called Zig and Zag and had Zig entered in a race in Shelbourne Park Dublin, a very big race. The day of the race arrived and they all drove to the track for a great night. However he arrived in Dublin with Zag. He had great hopes for that dog. During his time in the States he had to do national service and was sent to Germany and served his time in that country with Elvis Prestly, Mick said that he was a very quiet young lad. You may ask why he was called Kojack, It was because he resembled bald Telly Savalas of the TV programme. Another time he went to a funeral in America and did not come back for 9 months, his wife was in Poulmucka and she was American.

THINGS PEOPLE SAY

A Tall person

His head is a long way from the ground.

Small Person.

His arse is very near the ground.

Amadan,fool.

If he had twice as many brains he would still be a half wit.

Sickly person.

The weight of his piss is killing him and the heat of it is keeping him alive.

Sickly person.

Another clean shirt will do him.

Habitual liar

He thinks the truth is a secret.

A mean man.

As tight as a crabs arse. He has his Communion Money.

Alcoholic

He likes a pint or he has been known to take a drink.

A tough man to make a bargain.

The softest part of him is his National Health false teeth.

Sensible Person.

The next mistake he makes, will be his first.

Not feeling good

I'm as weak as a traitnin.

A good looking man or woman going out for the night.

If she was a bar of chocolate she would eat herself.

Never ask a child who his father is, he may not know. Always ask who his mother is, he is bound to know.

A LOVING MOTHER

They're all out of step except my Johnnie.

Drill Sergeant.

You broke your mothers heart, you will not break mine.

A badly reared young lad.

The mother would be better off if she had a bag of coal.

False friend

My auld segosha.

Notions.

A ha'penny looking down on a penny.

Optimist

His glass is always half full.

Pessimist.

His glass is always half empty.

Liar.

The truth is never a barrier to him.

THE GOOD OLD DAYS

Landlord showing off at a party he gives, even though he is broke. He instructs the servant to bring the best wine, the servant returns with the wine and the Landlord asks if this is the best wine? The servant answers no sire …but it is the best you've got.

Later that night the Landlord argues with his son in the presence of the guests and threatens to cut him out of his will with only a penny. Where are you going to get a penny? asks the son.

THE BEST OF TIMES

Jerry O' Donoghue one night in a singing lounge said to a long legged woman,,I would guess that you are a good singer … .Why do you say that says she…Because you have legs like a sparrow. On another night in the same lounge he went into the event with a ferret and left him off.

The ensuing scene was similar to that of Pompeii in the last few minutes.

CHERNOBYL

I am reminded of a conversation that I had with my good friend Johnny Burke, a man not known for pulling his punches, around the time that Irish families were taking in some of the unfortunate children for a short period into their own homes. This was around 1987 or 1989. One family that housed the children would not have been the best parents in the world and were hardly able to look after their own, but political pull or just downright bad decisions won out in the end. When Johnny heard this he remarked that the children were better off in Chernobyl. Johnny and his family for years and years after were hosts to a little Russian girl when the others had given up.

SYMPATHY FOR THE DYING

In the year 1999 I had the misfortune of going through heart bypass surgery, everything did not go as planned, there were a few hiccups with the recovery and it took a little longer than usual. I was in an induced coma for a week and of course the first report of my death went out. I was in the intensive care ward for a few weeks and eventually began to recover. There were about five lines coming out of me into various machines, I did not look good. My sons Waylon 16 and Emmet 14 at that time came to visit me. After a few minutes Waylon asked if I was going to die, and Emmet asked straight after …can I have the Car.?

BRIDIE

Before she left her native village of Doon she was known a Biddy Woods, but in Cahir following her marriage to Matt Lonergan she became Bridie Lonergan, The Irish name for Doon is Doon Bleisce and as any Gaelgoir will tell you that it means Whores Fort. Outsiders tried to change the name but the natives insisted it remains so.

THE LAST WOLF

Many counties all over the island claim to have been the last refuge of the Irish wolf. In almost every county there is a Wolf Hill or Hollow. It was widely believed that the last wolf that was in Tipperary, was killed in the Knockmealdown Mountains above Clogheen in the year 1770. It was said that he was hunted down with Wolfhounds because he was killing sheep. It has been mooted about the Wolf making a return to the mountains. I wonder if the sheep farmers and mountain walkers have an opinion on this..

SEAN SEIPEAL

Newcastle has a fascinating holy well called Sean Seipeal nesting on the foothills of the Knockmealdowns. It means old church and indeed the penal times saw it being used as a place to say mass. There is a little road down to the well and the congregation used to gather there. The priest used to say mass on a small clearing and if the British found them on the clearing as mass was being said, they would be punished, but if they were on the pathway outside the wall, nothing could be done to them. There are two fresh water springs adjacent to a little river that runs down along into the Suir.

Not far from the well is Mulloch Abbey founded in 1200 by Augustinian Nuns and is actually a Nunnery.

There are 12 Townlands in Newcastle

Aughavanlomaun…Boolahallagh…Clashavougha…Clashganny East

Clashganny West…Crohan… Curraghcloney …Garryduff.

Kilnacarriga…Middlequarter… Priestown..Rossmore.

The village is the starting point for hill or mountain walkers and of course every year there is the Liam Lynch commemeration at the monument.

Newcastle was home to several Irish Music pipers and Irish dancers and is reported to be an Irish speaking village.

NEW INN IN 1899

This is said of New Inn in 1889.That it was a village of 133 people.

New Inn is a pretty situated village on the side of a hill, 4 Irish miles North By East from Cahir and 4 miles south of Cashel and 9 miles northwest of Clonmel. It is in the barony of Middlethird and parish of Knockgraffon. The Sisters of Mercy, a branch from Charleville, have a convent here. They keep a select ladies school and teach under the National Board of Education. New Inn once had fairs, but none have been held for many years.The land of the district is good for pasture and tillage. Oats, potatoes and wheat are the principal crops. During the Geraldine League for maintaining Catholic rights in the reign of Elizabeth, the parish of Knockgraffon was the scene of a battle in which the Earl of Desmond gained a victory over the Anglo-Irish led by the Butlers, brothers of the Earl of Ormonde. About 3 miles from New Inn is the old Castle of Knockgraffon, belonging to Mr.Joseph Cooke and in the vicinity commanding a fine view of the Suir. There is a high earthen fort about 100 feet high, and is a favourite place for country dances.

Grocers and spirit dealers..Pat Barron and Ml. Tobin.

A WEDDING

Saturday 14 February 1942

The wedding was solemnised at Ballylooby church recently of Mr. Patrick Slattery, son of Mrs. Margaret Slattery, Rehill, Ballylooby, and Miss Peggy Tobin, daughter of Mrs, Nora Tobin and the late David Tobin, Rehill. The ceremony with Nuptial Mass was performed by the Rev. D. Slattery CC, Dunhill, brother of the bridegroom, assisted by Rev. T. Tobin CC, Lismore { cousin }. The bridegroom is well known in Gaelic circles, being Captain of the Rehill Hurling Club. The bride is also very popular in the district and is a first cousin of the Mayor of Boston, Maurice Tobin.

This account was from the Nationalist and Munster Advertiser.

CHERNOBYL CHILDREN'S PROJECT

The greatest disaster of our time happened on the 26th April 1986.The Chernobyl Nuclear Reactor exploded with devastating effect on the people for thousands of miles around. Most Countries went to help and supply aid to the misfortunate people.

Easter Sunday 1999 a convoy of three trucks and eight ambulances with Cahir Volunteers Gerry Niland, Jim O Rourke and Louise Reidy set off with equipment and medical supplies for the Orphanages that were in the affected regions. Besides Gerry, Jim and Louise the Cahir Committee were Marie Niland, Kay Hickey and Ellen and Kevin Hubbard.

The unknown beckons with a Journey of 3.500 Kms ahead. The week-long trek was spent sleeping in the ambulances and trucks as well as cooking on camping equipment and everything was in tins.

Leaving Cahir and heading for Dublin to England and going through France, Belgium, Germany, Poland and Ukraine. The horror that the volunteers experienced on arrival in the orphanages and abandoned baby homes was a shock to any human being. In the plains of the Ukraine, the convoy was visited by wild bears at night in search of food. The volunteers brought little presents for the Russian volunteers like Easter Eggs that the natives never saw before. The Russian red tape was a hindrance at every checkpoint, it did not seem to matter that these volunteers were there to help. All the equipment and the medical supplies as well as the ambulances were a result of fundraising locally.

For anyone to put themselves through the horror of that journey deserves the highest respect.

That same year 20 children from the Chernobyl region were put up by Host families around Cahir for a month. The convoy was full of vital medicines that were donated locally. Gerry Niland said …the sight of the inside of an abandoned baby home and an orphanage will forever stay with him……babies with their brain outside of their head, legless and armless babies and worse.

A LABOURER KILLED AT A WEDDING

New york February 1897

A fatal occurrence is reported from Ballylooby, County Tipperary.

During the wedding festivities of an army pensioner named Philip Smith on Thursday night, a party of young men from Clogheen who were present, resented the intrusion of another party from the immediate neighbourhood. A row eventually ensued. Patrick Doody, a labourer aged 26, received a blow from a stone to the head and died as a result.

Two men of the Clogheen party…Thomas Flynn and James Barrett have been arrested on a charge of causing Doody's death. At the inquest Saturday on the deceased the jury, in accordance with the doctor's evidence, said that the death was due to injuries to the brain caused by the great violence received.

Chauncey M. Depew

New York Saturday.

THE ARCADIA

A short term dance licence in respect of the new Arcadia Ballroom Barrack Road Cahir, which it was stated would hold 1400 people, was granted by Justice Skinner at Cahir Court. The licence will operate from December 13, opening night, 1963 to January 1964.

Mr. A. O'Dwyer solicitor Cahir for the applicant, Con Hynes, Abbey Street Portumna, said that the hall was not fully completed but he was willing to give an undertaking that the requirements would be fulfilled before opening. Mr.B. Maguire solicitor for the South Tipperary County Council said that they would have no objection if the Fire Chiefs requirements were fulfilled. Inspector B.Lynch raised the question of parking and was given an undertaking that everything would be ready for the night, the Arcadia drew a lot of business to the bars around town. all the towns for a 30 mile radius had buses and coaches coming every weekend. Report from the Nationalist.

BALLYLOOBY TOWNLANDS

Poulaculleare   Quarry Hole.

Burgess and West Burgess.

Parkaderreen   Little field of the Oaks.

Curraghtoor.

Burgess Mansion.

Scartana   Anne's Thicket.

Knockane   Small hill.

Kilroe   Red Church.

Clogheenafishoge   Little stone of the fairies.

Rehill   An Rechoill   .The grove.

Whitechurch.

Burgess New.

Kilcoran   Cuarains Church.

Derravoher   Oak road.

Ballyallavoe   Holloways glen.

Poulavalla   Holloways hole.

Moanroe   Red bog.

Knockanegurm   Little blue hill.

CLOGHEEN TOWNLANDS

Ballyboy

Canroe

Drumlemmin

Graigue

Garrymore

Shanrahan

Rearoe

Flemingstown

Carriganroe.

Carrigmore

Shanbally

Cranna

Coolville

Clashleigh

Castlegrace

Killballyboy

Gortacullen

Curraghclooney

Shanbally

Ballyverassa

Bohernagore

Ballinhalla

Ballynomasna

Parsons Green

Coolbawn

Inchnamuck

Glencallaghan

Killeaton

Clogheen Cottage Hospital was kept in operation by the local people, when the Government of the day wanted to close all such Hospitals in the country.

TITHE WARS 1830-1836

The tithe wars were a nonviolent action taken against British rule, although there were sporadic outbreaks around the country. The tithes were a tax imposed on Catholics for the upkeep of the established church which was Protestant. Goods were seized in lieu of non payment. The Catholics refused to bid at any auction where their countrymens goods were up for sale.

On the 9 th June 1836 the Fennels of Rehill who were a Quaker family refused to pay and as a result some of their goods were seized and put for auction. There was a tithe agent who lived in Cahir town called

Long-Jim Beere and the Parson from Tubrid called Palmer were the only two bidders at the auction of a carriage and horse. The prize fell to the Parson for £23- 5s. having paid part of what was owed. The total that was owed was £43, The local Catholics flatly refused to take part in any auction.

WEALTHY MARRIAGE IN 1890

Samuel Burke's seventh daughter was married to M.Purcell, a solicitor from Macroom. Samuel was from Kilemny. Cahir. The wedding was private and the presents were published in the National papers, here are some of the gifts. From the bridegroom. A diamond and sapphire ring, a diamond and ruby ring and a diamond sapphire bracelet in a dressing bag. The fathers of both bride and groom gave a cheque. The best man gave a lovely set of Dessert knives and spoons and it goes on..a complete dinner service….silver teapot…a hand painted fire screen and afternoon tea cloth…an opera glass..a feather fan…dinner gong and a set of chimes..a picnic basket…silver afternoon tea set….case of perfume…a pretty opera cloak…a statue and a very pretty chair back. A case of books..a lobster salad bowl…an ink stand…a handsome brooch…cut glass and silver claret jugs..silver toast rack..Pearl and gold bracelet. The staff presented the pair with a silver salad bowl. The bridegroom presented the bridesmaids with gold pearl swallow brooches………..The opera cloak was very thoughtful.

THE CLOGHEEN MINES.

The population of Clogheen in 1881 was 1209 but that does not reflect the amount of business that was carried on in the town, the town was one of the best business towns in Tipperary. There was talk of running a railway link from Cahir, but it never came to fruition. At one time there were 4 flour mills and three hotels and well stocked shops and a brewery.

The British army barracks had accomodation for a Captain and two Lieutenants as well as 50 personnel. The market house was destroyed by fire and never rebuilt. A pig fair took place every third Monday and the cattle fair lost out to competition from Cahir and Mitchelstown.

In the 1780s there was a profitable Silvermine at Castlegrace. It is not recorded why it closed. It was found that the Knockmealdowns were rich in iron. There were several woollen mills that were busy because of the British waging war in other countries.

Whiteboyism was rife in this part of the country and it was said that every youth was enrolled and was eager to do so. This was one of the reasons that Fr. Sheehy was hanged on a trumped up charge.

The ambitious Clogheen Nationalists were hatching a plot to bring French troops to fight the British. The business people had gas lights erected around the town at their own expense and they maintained them. There were 14 Sisters that taught in the schools and the others worked in the Union Hospital, otherwise known as the Poorhouse the Poor Law Union had its headquarters in Clogheen, this was a refuge for the destitute especially during the great hunger. The author of this book has more than a passing affair with Clogheen. My grandfather was married in the poorhouse in 1918. My father died in the hospital and I was born there in October 1949. In the days when the Labour Party had a strong branch in Cahir, we used to meet with the Clogheen branch in Lawlors pub, the pub was quaint and was never modernised but retained the old look that can never be replicated.

CAHIR DRAMATIC SOCIETY

This article was written by Ernie Alton for the centenary of the Nationalist Newspaper in 1990.

The demise of touring companies encouraged amateur theatre. Cahir Muintir na Tire Club based in Cahir Castle presented numerous one -act plays, variety programmes and a memorable production of Many Young Men of Twenty by John B Keane. The club's production team included Sean Walsh, Michael Regan and Pat Burke.

Cahir Dramatic Society was formed in the early 50s at a meeting called by the disbanding Gaelic League Branch. There are no records extant, but from memory those present were James Gogarty, Mary Irwin, Liam P O'Connor, Michael Downes, Noel Fitzgerald, John Joe Brookes and Ernest V Alton. It was agreed to transfer the assets to the new group.

Launched with an ambitious choice of Arrah Na Pogue with multiple scene changes and period costumes, the Society presented 36 other plays in succeeding years. Opting for a wider audience they entered the competitive drama festival circuit in 1958, building a reputation as one of the leading groups in the country.

Many would rate… The Black Stranger …by Denis Healy, Produced by Patrick J Walsh in 1961 as the best of many excellent productions.

Hilton Edwards said of it …I think this is one of the best amateur performances I have seen, I never thought I would be able to say that. I really would put on this play for anyone, anywhere. With this cast and this producer I feel privileged to have seen it. The production was placed third in the all Ireland that was held in Athlone. Others to receive the prestigious nominations were..No

Home Tomorrow written and produced by Paddy Walsh 1963 and All The King's Horses by John Mc Donnell produced by Michael Regan. 1977.

Ernest V Alton was a Post Office official and was Chairman of the Labour Party Branch in Cahir. He was also a candidate in 1991 for the Council Elections and narrowly defeated by 21 votes.

RECOLLECTIONS

E.V.Alton.

School days shade all too quickly into new horizons, a first dance in the hall of the Old Barracks in Kilcommon, with Kevin Flynn and the band and what could be more romantic than oil lamps hanging from the rafters. Later one graduated to the Parochial hall with Mick Dennehy and his band or The Twilight Serenaders. Later still to the Galtee Hotel where the enterprising proprietor Jack Kennedy engaged leading bands like Johnny Dankworth, Joe Loss and Edmondo Ross. Peggy Dell was a regular. The Arcadia of course flourished in the 60s as a commercial chain.

The Emergency was endured like an unwelcome guest. Rationing shortages and brown bread and a half ounce of tea were part of a wide range of restrictions. Domestic fuel was scarce and some genius came up with a sawdust fire. If the sawdust was dry everything was alright but if the material was wet then the trouble began. Another thing that was in short supply was cigarettes and people tried to come up with substitute tobacco but to no avail. The black market was in full swing, today's health warnings did not exist and a lot of effort went into acquiring a smoke. As far as the smoker was concerned it was F,,, you Jack.

Baff Carew in the Square was a tobacconist who held open house as long as stocks lasted, In order to stretch supplies you might be offered three normal cigs and seven inferior ones. There was a cigarette called White Horse and it was like smoking turf.

The 13th Battalion stationed in Cahir Abbey and on the grounds of the old British army barracks established a good rapport with the community and a welcome boost to the economy. Some stayed on when they were disbanded, contributing to the social and commercial life of the town.

Peter Riordan was one that stayed on, a great man to put a story together, always immaculately dressed. Peter's wife Gerty had a hairdressing salon on barrack street and was a great favourite with women of a certain age. Bridie Lonergan was one of the blue rinse brigade.

MEMORIES

Asking different people around the town what they remembered most about times gone by.

All seem to remember the good summers when they were young. Going swimming at the Sandy Bottom and the Sandy Bank and the trips to Clonea and Tramore. Some of the older people were singing the praises of the Mystery Tours and the train trips. Every year there was a train trip to the Isle Of Man. Going to the island and back on the same day. When you made your Communion it was a trip to Woolworths in Clonmel.

Picking the whorts on the mountain for a pittance and getting bitten by bugs and horse flys was no joke. In winter skating on ponds that now no longer are there. When the Circus came to town and saw Tom Hubbard in the Circus band for the day. Those of a religious bent remember the Corpus Christie parades when the whole town turned out, you could not see the Square because of the amount of people. A farmer said that the street fairs were the highlight of his youth. On our way to school we had to avoid the cow dung all the way across town. Before they built the Cattle Mart in 1957 this was the scene every month. Without a doubt the one that came up most was the Capitol Cinema and the matinee every Sunday and hoping that there was going to be a cowboy film, a western.

There were dancing in the Parochial Hall and the Castle before the Arcadia. There were always two sides to the town and the children did different things to amuse themselves. On our side we used to slide down the railway embankment on cardboard boxes or go on trips up the mountain. Our parents never worried about us because the country was a safer place. There used to be Gymkhanas in the Inch Field as well as soccer tournaments like the pub leagues, the Cahir Dramatic Society put on plays and were always packed. Street corners were a favourite meeting place to catch up on the latest scandal. The handball alley was a busy place all year round. The singing lounges like Phil Boyles and the Silver sands were very enjoyable. These were the best of times.

CAN'T ARGUE WITH THAT

Almost everybody dislikes England and that opened the debate about the European Cup. The scene was Meads pub on Barrack Street. Ireland were playing Denmark and our chances were being discussed by Paddy Saunders and a few more. Paddy lived for these debates and was seldom on the sensible side. He let it be known that he hated the Danes because of what they did the last time they came over to Ireland. Someone asked what did they do ?.The answer was ..They killed Brian Boru.

On another occasion Peter Riordan was having a stand up row with a man that had just returned from England and on a pension. The row was getting very heated and Peter thought it wise to withdraw, as he reached the door he turned to fire his parting shot. He said ..say what you like about me Davy boy..but I never sucked the Queens diddy.

One of Archie Condons customers had suffered a stroke but he managed to get to the pub every night, he was a whiskey drinker and his body was bent and twisted as well as being on the wrong side of 80. Archie, as Jerry was known, had a habit of buying some drinks at bargain prices. He bought a consignment of Red Hackle Scotch Whiskey, a drink that was less than popular. A new customer asked for a scotch and Jerry asked if Red Hackle would do…the customer asked if it was a good whiskey and Jerry pointed to the stroke victim and said that it was the best because .. look what it did to him.

Fergie Bell's uncle Jimmy died and was to be buried in the Kilcommon Cemetery, Fergie and myself volunteered to dig the grave but there was a bottle of whiskey and some beer which rendered us incapable, we had about half of the dept of the hole dug that evening when Mick Vincent appeared and said…get out of it or we will be here till doomsday.

DAUGHTERS OF DUN IASCAIGH

This is a group of women in Cahir that are interested in History and promoting the contribution that women have made to the town.

They were National Heritage Winners in 2021.

In Cahir the group has erected 27 blue circular plaques to recognise the effort that women have through the ages endured.

Every year the group holds a Wuthering Heights event in the Hotel or Inch field and is growing every year.

The participants dress in red costumes and are joined by some male friends. Josephine O'Neill seems to be at the helm and is always at the forefront of the action.

JILL AND DAN

Our dog had seven puppies, mostly black and tan

Daddy sold them all but two, we called them Jill and Dan

They were as fat as lumps of butter, all huddled in a heap.

Whenever we took a look at them, they were always fast asleep.

The mothers not all that friendly now, though extra good to eat.

If we go too near the puppies, she shows two big white teeth.

We took the mother for a walk, while daddy docked the pups.

Mummy said twas cruelty, Daddy said whist up

Now we hurry home from school, to play with Jill and Dan.

We run and hide or climb the slide, tis catch me if you can.

We're all proud of daddy, he's what you call a man.

Despite some tempting offers, he won't sell Jill and Dan.

The late Bill O. from New Inn who once had a coal store in Abbey Street he smoked a pipe and played the banjo. His full title was The Bill O'Connor, brother to the late Paddy O.

Letter written by Jonathan Hill to William Going on March 18th 1817. Looking for advice about a certain woman. The letter was found when the Mill was between owners. 1962

My dear William.

My delay in replying to thy letter of the 26th did not proceed from want of feeling the most lively interest to one of the matters of which thou write,

And with thou future welfare is so intimately connected, but from a variety of harassing cares which continually intruded so as scarcely to allow a moment to myself.

I shall however now dismiss them, and state to thee in words, the sentiment of which I have so often in person so frequently impressed upon thee, being altogether uninfluenced by any feelings in the business but that which friendship and affection should dictate.

From the slight acquaintance I have with our fair friend, she appears to me to be one with whom her equal in society, provided he felt for her a sincere attachment, might with great confidence risk the fortunes of his life, For with little prospect of myself being married, I am a warm advocate of the conjugal for I reverence, as I ought, that mysterious union of soul and body which binds the husband to the wife by ties more indissoluble than laws can possibly create. And in order to make this state such as Providence intended it there should be a congeniality of soul joined to the most pure and distinguished heart.

I believe that affection and naturally good understanding,

A great deference to the opinion of each other, but above all a cheerful agreeable temper are necessary ingredients for a happy and conjugal state, my judgement much misleads me if the person in question is deficient in any of these respects, but which, before thou commit thyself

In the slightest degree, prudence will require thee to industriously to ascertain.

A father who knew the world well once told his daughter that she should be extremely cautious in letting her husband know the extent of her affection as little further was then left for him to discover. The same advice applies in my mind, to our own sex .

And there is no one thing in this world men are more likely to be deceived than when they judge from appearance that their love is returned. There are a thousand circumstances that render it the interest of the female to make you imagine your attentions are agreeable, and by such artifices you are insensibly led on until you become completely enslaved.

Perhaps this caution is unnecessary to thee, From one who was once deceived, the first time you are deceived it is the fault of those that deceived you, but if you are deceived a second time the fault is thine own.

I was almost going to say were I in thy circumstances I should not hesitate a moment in mentioning the matter to my uncle and aunt,

But then many things are to be considered, thy college and studies and the want of knowing anything of the sentiments of our fair friend. It is impossible to give correct advice so be guided by thine own feelings do not suffer heated and tumultuous thoughts to displace cool reflection. I do not think thy uncle and aunt should know immediately if thy mind is fully made up, secrecy is indispensable. But by all means seek to find the lady's thoughts by privately conferring with her on the subject prior to her father being told.

When may I look for you in the city ?.

I remain,dear William

Thy most affectionate friend

Jonathan Hill.

Now that's how a Quaker gives advice.

Seanie Lonergan

THE TOWN HALL CLOCK

By John Quirke Jeweller.

I started my business as a Jeweller/Watchmaker in Cahir in 1976 on Church Street. I then moved to Number 1 Old Church Street, on the corner of the Clonmel road opposite the old County Council offices and the old Library and Courthouse.

One evening the Librarian, Jack Doherty rushed into the shop and asked if I could fix the clock on the tower above the roof of the building. This clock it seems had not worked properly for years. At the request of the Tipperary County Council, Hally Brothers had been contracted to re - roof the building and also to remove the clock, the tower and the weather vane.

We were asked to see if we could repair the clock. When the clock was taken down for inspection it was in pretty poor condition as it had been exposed to all kinds of weather, not to mention insects,vermin and birds.

Brendan Kerins, my brother in law, worked with me at the time so we took on the job of taking the electric movement apart and cleaned and oiled all the wheels and moving parts. We had a deadline of about 10 days to complete the job. After doing all we could,

We re-assembled it all and polished it up and were pleasantly surprised when the clock started to go again despite it showing signs of wear and tear. The weather vane which sat on top of the tower above the clock was also in very bad condition and local blacksmith / ironmonger, the late Patrick Burke, the forge, on the Clonmel road repaired and repainted it to its former glory.

The clock was offered back up to the tower and was now better protected by its new roof. The weather vane was also installed on top of the tower where it sits proudly today.

Each of these jobs at the time were done by Patrick Burke and John Quirke Jeweller free of charge to the Tipperary County Council.

We also recognise that due to the intervention of Jack Doherty, Librarian

this project would not have been completed and another landmark would have been lost forever.

The clock ran pretty well for nearly 30 years from its last complete service until its complete demise as the old electric movement had completely worn out beyond repair. We then tried a new industrial quartz movement but this was not powerful enough to carry the large hands.

At this stage I had moved the shop in 1991 to my present location,14 Castle Street. People kept ringing me to ask when I was going to fix the clock as it was part of the history and landmark of the town. With expert advice and the help of Philip Stokes, master clockmaker in Cork city, we sourced an industrial clock movement. With full cooperation of the county Council and Mary Lonergan Butler, the next step was to restore the tower which housed the clock movement. This was done by carpenter Martin Halpin who obtained the perspex. The clock was rewired by local electrician Dan Casey. The new complete clock had to be hoisted by lift to its present position, a landmark once again.

The novelty of this modern clock movement, it automatically changes time by satellite forward from Winter to Summer Time in April and back again to Winter time in October. As the years roll by it will continue to do so. Unlike the old clock movement which had to be controlled manually by electric switch a few times a year. If there was a power outage it had to be set by Ann Simpson Tuohy Librarian. Anne was a great guardian of the clock

So when you look up and read the time on the clock, see which way the wind is blowing, from the weather vane, think of the story behind these landmarks and the people that keep them here.

Tempus Fugit.

John Quirke.

SEAN O'DOMHNAILL, B,1873,SCART NA NGLEOBHRAN,

Ballylooby, Cahir Co.Tipperary.

Lord Waterpark had a storehouse built beside our village in which he stored corn and other farm produce that he confiscated from his tenants as payment for their rents. Waterparks agent O'Brien, looked after the sale of confiscated goods. This agent is still remembered in our parish for his infamous treatment of the absentee landlords tenants.

A quaker settler, Jackson by name, was kinder to his neighbours.He does not appear to be a landlord. He spoke Irish fluently and helped the Famine victims by giving them plots of potatoes and free milk.

A further incident which happened about 1852 illustrated the harshness of the masters of the people in those days. My great grandfather and my great grandmother were employed by estate agent Jellico to gather weeds in cishes [baskets] as a method of cleaning the land. Jellico stood watching the operations. In the evening they had collected a few small potatoes [criochain] for themselves. He, having seen this, harshly ordered them to forfeit these seemingly useless potatoes. They received 4d each per day.

On another occasion he granted them, with other workmen, a half day to go to Cahir town to see the execution of two men who had been convicted of stealing some timber from a local wood. 'Twill teach ye to obey the law' he remarked.

THE QUAKER BURIAL GROUND RULES

It is directed that the stones to be used shall not exceed thirty inches in length and twenty four in breath, and that the inscription shall be in plain roman letters. The inscription is confined to a simple record of the deceased. The object in this instance being simply that of defining the position of the grave. To the satisfaction of surviving relatives.

PATRICK KELLY

He's sleeping in a hero's grave,

Beside the town of Cahir,

Who was the bravest of the brave,

Of courage true and rare,

He gave his life – he did his best,

To save a neighbours child,

And bring her to her mothers breast,

From water raging wild,

And though he struggled but in vain,

To save the child from death,

His story will be told again,

By those unborn yet,

He honour brought his fellow man,

Both here and every place,

Such deeds as Patrick Kelly's can,

Exalt the human race.

Composed by John Daly of Clogheen .

CAHIR MILLS SILO

In 1935 a new 1000 - ton Grain Silo was erected on the other side of the road from the mill. Grain was transported across by a worm conveyor to the mill. This worm conveyor was dismantled in 1985. The silo in its time had a state of the art wheat cleaning and drying machinery, coupled with the storage facilities at Cahir Abbey Mills. Church Street Stores enabled the firm to store the region of 90,000 barrels of grain. Following the mill closure the silo fell into disuse for many years and became a health hazard. The asbestos lagging was being blown out the broken windows and found its way around town. Seanie Lonergan led a successful campaign to have the silo removed.

SUSPENSION OF A QUAKER

February 1843 the quarterly meeting of the Society of Friends assembled at Cork, has an appeal confirmed, the decision of the Clonmel and Cahir monthly meeting in suspending Samuel Jellico of Cahir, agent to the Earl of Glengall. Because he paid tithe rent charge on His Lordships property to the parochial incumbent, the Friends being totally averse to all ecclesiastical demands.

Richard Grubb, his wife Susan and their family, purchased Cahir Abbey.

The Abbey, its mills and the land from the executors of the Fennels.

The property of Cahir Abbey was between 750 and 1000 acres of land.

Fishing rights on the river Suir, valuable frontage of ½ mile on both sides of the Tipperary - Cahir road, front and back of river lodge cottages-two barrack like semi detached houses double fronted between the mill and the main road, tennis courts and walled gardens –- and so these mills became the property of the Grubbs.

Richard Grubb took little interest in the mills and left the running of them to Richard Junior and his partner Bancroft. Richard lived in the barracks and Bancroft lived next door.

In 1844 they countenanced music and dancing and they were disowned by the Society of Friends at a meeting in November 1844. This appeared to have no effect on their milling ability as Richard [junior] immersed himself into the work of the mills and was employing an increasing number of hands. Bancroft had six sons employed as managers and they were content with their work. Richard moved from Cahir Abbey in 1863 and surrendered all his interest in the mills to his brother.

One of Richard's sons, Frederick, married Edith Going and moved into the Barrack house vacated by Richard when he moved from Cahir Abbey. The houses on the left of the mill lane were called Barrack houses. The second house on the Tipperary side was for a good many years St. Joseph's college.

THE BALLYMURPHY WOMAN

She came to Cahir from Ballymurphy Co. Carlow in the 60s to work in the Cahir House Hotel and did so for a short time, Anyone that worked in the hotel at that time would not have a good word for Bumps as she was called. Following a term at the Limerick Inn, she returned to the Galtee Hotel and in later years to the Galtee Inn. She met and married Paddy Roche and had a family Mary, Margaret, Padraig, and Aine. Liz worked with my wife Margaret and when Mag was sick Liz was always there. She used to walk out to my house several times every week, a distance of 5 Kilometres with her little dog. Liz had a great sense of humour and was a great worker. When she got the bad news, her son Paudie brought his wedding date nearer so Liz could attend. Her final days in November 2005 were spent in the hospice and with only days to go, I sat on the bed and said …Liz I would have bet any money that you would bury me…….don't talk too soon she said. Such was her sense of humour. Liz left a memory on everyone that knew her, a great friend and a great neighbour.

MELISSA HILL

Another Cahir girl that made it to the big time, is the author Melissa Hill, daughter of Nell and Noel Fitzgerald of Pearce street. Melissa is a USA Today and Irish Times bestselling author, her books have been translated into twenty six languages and is the author of ten bestsellers.

Melissa says that she enjoys writing immensely but it is a solitary profession and as long as inspiration is still with her she will continue to write. We wish her all the success.

THE WILD ROVERS

GAA. Cahir hurling going back a few years there were 5 Moloney brothers with the Wild Rovers and the Slashers in 1969, the Moloney brothers hailed from Poulmucka.

ABBEY STREET 1968

Growing up on Abbey Street you had Upper and Lower. Starting at the lower end was Jackie Nolans shop. This shop had a jukebox and was a great meeting place for the youth. The Supervalue shop is there now. Next to Nolans was Slattery's Hardware, a corrugated iron structure painted green. Next to that was the river and then Barry's Garage with Jimmy Nugent and Terry O Connor, mechanics. It was a Morris and Austin motor car dealer. Behind the garage was the town dump. The other side of the road began with the Bridge House pub and next to that the second shop was Billy Roche who had a sweet shop. Across the bridge was the original Black Toms, a pub and grocery shop and across from the pub, was a little farmyard and milking parlour. There was also a hay barn which was a much used spot for courting couples. Liam Lonergan had a shop. Above that was a grain store and beside that was Hugh Coyle, a shoemaker. Next to that was Colton's Bar and grocery and restaurant. The Bill O' had a coalstore underneath the Boxing Club. A door or two above that was Sergeant O'Halloran.

Starting at the mountain road corner was Mary Bestons hairdressing and Mrs.Ford's hairdresser shop and along was the Kickham Press now defunct. Beary's Garage was next, run by the Captain who never left the army. He marched at top speed everywhere. He sold petrol and a range of parts for cars as well as Ding Dong Hacksaws, Gandy fan belts and Whoosh tyres. He raced Go Karts and rode scrambler motorbikes. He went up the river in a boat made from an aeroplane fuel tank, bawling orders in nautical terms.

Next to Bearys was old Ernie Bates who was a Blueshirt and his wife was a staunch Republican. Ernie was an old school french polisher. The next shop was Mrs. Keating draper and Mrs. Devereux, a sweet and tobacco shop. Towards Tipperary was Ladrigans wonderful shop that sold top class produce. The last shop on Upper Abbey Street was Dan Crowley, a grocery shop. You had to travel a little further up the road to get to the Handy Shop, another shop that stayed open very late.

This shop was owned by the Fleming family.

THE PETROL PUMP

As we stand in 2024 there are 4 filling stations in the town, In the sixties there were petrol pumps all around town, that means that there are tanks buried all over. There were two petrol pumps outside

Bearys and another two on the footpath outside Barry's Garage. There was another outside Sunderlands pub as well as a pair outside Burke's arch in the Square.

Another stood at Franklin's pub and Condons and another at the corner of Market Street and outside the Galtee Inn. We had only a few cars on the road and had five times the petrol pump count.

SAWMILLS

In the sixties there were several sawmills in the town's vicinity. Hallys had a sawmill on the Clonmel road just above the old Church. This was a large affair managed by a man called Malachy. I remember Sean Ryan and his brother Mattie as well as Liam Loughman as truck driver, as I remember it was a very busy enterprise.

Jimmy Rankin had another saw mill and was widely regarded as a genius as far as timber was concerned. Jimmy had his mill for a time in the Erasmus School. Jimmy was constantly blinking from all his years on the saw.

The Cahir estate had several mills adjacent to the nearby woods; one of these was in Scarough wood. Jimmy Auld had his mill at Ballydrehid until recently. The cover in Garryroan was last cut in the late 50s by a huge firm at the time called McAinish, a firm from

Scotland. This is an area of 180 acres and is ready for harvesting again. It is of course a game reserve.

In the Cahir area now if you want saw mill cut timber you have Tobins mills in Rehill, a small family run operation. Pat Sheehans in Burncourt

Is the larger of the two, Sheehans is another family run mill and has been in operation a long time. The large mills like Glennons are the death knell for the smaller mills.

THE SEWING FACTORY

Another one of the oldies is the Sewing Factory that was in the old doctors surgery car park, the old market yard. At the time of its peak production it was owned by Jimmy Walsh of the Square. This Jimmy was Joe Walsh's grandfather. There were about 20 women employed there and they made all kinds of clothes, both womens and mens apparel.

Anne Doyle [Coffey] told me that she used to make trousers for a Garda in Cork as he would not go elsewhere for them. Jimmy could not drive as he had not got a car, he hired a car from O'Meara's a trucking firm on the Mitchelstown road, it was an old Mercedes and got Christy Doyle to drive him to Dublin looking for orders and buying cloth. If any one had a coat that was made in the factory the girls could tell who made it, they all knew each other's sewing.

The factory was sold to a man named Joe Boles and it stayed in operation for a short time afterwards. Some of the women that I can remember that worked there were. Anne Doyle..Dolores Morris..Mary Bridget Morris..Mary Keating..Breda Burke..Maggie Magner…Mrs

Maggie O'Connor.

THE WHITEBOYS

An agrarian organisation formed in South Tipperary in 1791 that campaigned against tithe collection and evictions and any injustice committed against the common man. The white boy tag came from the practice of wearing white masks, not unlike the Ku, Klux, Klan

There was no problem in getting recruits to exact revenge against British rule. The authorities called them Levellers because they took down fences and orchards belonging to anyone that paid tithes. Around Cahir, Clogheen and in Ballylooby they were especially active. Their membership increased and they were more violent and frequent. As time went on they rose to arson and even murder. In Loughkent cemetery there is a grave of 3 brothers in their 20s killed by the group for taking land that belonged to an evicted farmer.

FACTION FIGHTING

Co. Tipperary is credited with having instigated this activity. I hasten to call it a sport, although it probably started out as a game.

Whenever there was a gathering like a horse fair or a normal fair, it was destined to start. It started with families having a falling out and swelled to villages and towns all over Munster before spreading to the rest of the country. The local priest in Ardfinnan called a halt to the factions from Newcastle and Ballybacon. There is an account of a fighter saying that it was done for the sheer love of fighting.

Needless to say alcohol played a large part at these events, women were not excluded and could only join in if their spouse was not taking part. Whereas men had fighting sticks that could be made from any type of wood, Ash, Oak, Sycamore and seasoned up the wide chimney to make them even harder. The women used to put rocks in woollen socks and were most feared. The opposing factions had names such as the Shanavests or the Two Year Olds and the Three Year Olds. The Blues

were from Tipperary. At one gathering in Pallasgreen a man walked with his coat dragging on the ground behind him and invited someone to step on his coat. When his coat was stepped on, all hell broke loose. Both factions would stay at it till they had no strength to carry on or were injured. There were almost no court cases brought by the protagonists,

They wanted another day out. For obvious reasons the fights were ignored by the Police, the clergy always tried to intervene but to no avail.

At Ballyea Strand in Kerry there was a fight involving almost two thousand men and women and it ended with 16 dead and hundreds of broken bones. This did not end for another eighty years, they say that the last fight in Tipperary was at Cappawhite in 1887 when the leader called The Russian Buckley was killed, when they took on their arch enemies of the village of Doon. There was however a court hearing but there was no sympathy from the Judge he said a man with a weak skull has no place at a Faction Fight. In Ardfinnan the priest called the Lancers from Cahir Barracks to quell the violence and both factions joined forces and ran them off.

MISCARRIAGE OF JUSTICE

It seems that everyone in the vicinity knew that Harry Gleeson was innocent. There were seven thousand people that signed a petition for his reprieve, but the lawlords ignored it. Someone murdered Moll Carthy but it was Harry Gleeson who got the blame. The Bill O Connor that knew Harry called it a farcical trial and he was proved right many years later. There has been several books written on the subject and no one worked harder than Eddie Dalton, to prove Harry's innocence.

The trial was heard in February 1941 in Dublin, for some reason all the evidence was not used and the defence was frustrated. Harry was found guilty and hanged on the 23rd April 1941 in Mountjoy Prison.

Eddie Dalton led a group that were successful in 2015 getting a posthumous pardon for Harry. The pardon was signed by Michael D Higgins, the President of Ireland. Nine more years had to pass before Harry's remains were disinterred from the prison yard and brought back to his home in Tipperary at Holycross. The real culprit was never brought to justice and at the time somebody had to know. How could they live with themselves and let an innocent man go to the gallows.

THE SAFE HOUSE

A few miles outside Cahir on the Cork side in the Townland of Quarryhole is a house high up on the Galtee mountainside that was used as a safe house during the war of Independence. The location was perfect as a hideout and was used as a base to semaphore messages across the valley to Newcastle. It is well known that the likes of Dinny Lacey...Dan Breen...Seamus Robinson...Sean Treacy...Sean Hogan and anyone that was on the run from the British tyrants used this house. The news that the British were on the way would put the boys under no pressure, they would just hide in the heather a little way up.The semaphore went on above the

British heads, as the woman of the house placed the washing in a certain way on the line. Across the valley the Newcastlemen knew every move.

THE SWALLOW

Written by Rosalynd Hurst, formerly Palmer.

I was born in Cahir. In 1947, I left when I was five. When I say ..left..you must understand I was a swallow, and like all birds return every summer, swooping in like the birds, exploring the town, walking along the river, up the mountain, knowing I was home. Then, home was my grandparents house opposite the ball alley, and my grandfather was manager of the creamery. What few factored in was that I was obsessed with animals, dreamed of being a farmer, but most of all loved the horses and ponies I would see passing the house on the way to drop off milk at the creamery.

My grandmother had cats, solitary, hostile creatures. My first success at having a pet was doomed although I had practised around the age of three, taking an elderly greyhound for an amble to the Square. Then real hope. My granduncle was a monk and manager of the farm at Mount Melleray. On a visit he took me to see puppies ready to leave their mother and I returned with a struggling puppy to the collective horror of all the adults, While it was thought disrespectful to reject a gift from a monk, I knew as soon as the poor puppy was sick over everyone on the return to Cahir, that his time with me would be short lived. No, he could not return to England with us. So he went to a farm, retained the name I had given him and died a very elderly successful sheep dog.

THE DONKEY

It was during this time that I began to haunt the farmers coming into the creamery with small carts drawn by donkeys or ponies. Each morning there was a line, the milk dropped off for pasteurisation, whey, butter, cream collected on the way out.

I think I was about five years old and was down at the creamery by the line of waiting farmers.How or why I picked out Neddy I cannot tell. They say that all donkeys all look alike, but one day I walked up and gave him a stroke and that was it.

Each day I would search for him, have a treat for him, give him a pat.

His bemused owner, Billy Costello, standing by the wall would look on.

I heard him say I don't know how the child does it, I'd hardly know Neddy myself. I returned each year and by the time I was seven,

Billy let me drive Neddy homeward towards the Mountain Road.

It took a summer or two before my mother thought she'd check up on where her daughter would disappear to every morning.

I remember well the day that Billy invited us up to his new bungalow for tea. There was Neddy in the field trotting over when I called his name.

Billy's advice to my mother was to stand back…That old ass is a cross fellow that will take a bite out of you or a kick if you weren't looking,

But that child can do anything with him and he is as soft and gentle with her.

That was the last time that I saw Neddy.

THE WILL

Summer 1952, Returning home.I learnt that Billy had died. I was very sad.

Billy was a lovely, kind man. Questions about the fate of Neddy were met with evasion. The farmers were now going to the creamery in trucks or the milk lorry was making the rounds of the farms, life in Cahir was on the change. It took me ten weeks of persistence for my aunt to tell me that it was Billy's wish that I should have Neddy. Was it a will, was it legal.? No reply, I dreamed of ways of getting him back to England but received no support. I was devastated. I am sure that if it was now, I would have merited expensive counselling, for no one would tell me where he had gone. Neddy was lost but not forgotten.

THE HEREAFTER

Swallows, they say, live to a great age travelling thousands of miles to Cahir, year after year,returning to Africa when Summer ends.

Me too no longer a child, no longer a young woman. Not so long ago, A summer and I was home. I took my favourite walk up the Mountain Road, with a friend, stopping to look back at the view.

That's where Billy's house was..I said.

He often talked about you and his donkey. she said.

I was ten when he died, I was so sad.

He's buried in the field there.

I mean I know in England there are many strange burials in weird places. But here in Cahir it's unbelievable I gasped.

Billys not in the churchyard. ?

What are you saying, Neddy your donkey. We looked after him for years.

Why did no one tell me?

A Laugh.

We were all sworn to silence. But you know we think he must have been

Over 50 when he died, stubborn wasn't the word. But my mother, who was fond of you, promised she would care for the donkey and he outlived her.

So Neddy had been there during all my years of visits, well cared for, though never taken to England by a lonely little girl. In the churchyard

I mourn and visit all the graves of those I knew and loved.

There is one walk up the Mountain Road that is always taken, and a stop by a field and a memory of a kindly old man and a stubborn old donkey, never forgotten.

Rosalynd's aunt Myr Kennedy lived to be 102 years. She left Cahir all those years ago and never failed to return and meet with everyone almost every year. She entered politics and was a Councillor for many years. When Rosalind is not …at home…

She keeps in touch with everybody that she knows. Thanks to the advent of Facebook she can keep her finger on the pulse. especially on People from Cahir on Facebook.

PADDY MAHON

I met up with Paddy in June of 2024 the first time in almost 60 years, the last time that I saw him he was playing for Cahir Park. A tall imposing man that came from Bengurrah. Paddy was the youngest of ten children.

Leaving school with a primary education he led a charmed and interesting life. He travelled all around the globe in many different guises.

Before he left he worked from a very young age at different short term jobs for farmers and the like. Just over his back wall was Bengurrah House owned at that time by Jacky Connors, who gave him work for the harvest season, he remembers Jacky's wife bringing the tea for the men in a bucket and big bacon sandwiches, at dinner they went up to the house for more bacon and cabbage. They worked hard at the hay and in the evening the woman of the house brought a bucket of Guinness which was very welcome.

He worked as a barman at the Galtee Inn for Tommy Kennedy and the Galtee Hotel for Jacky Kennedy from 1955 to 1957, and left when he got a job as a barman in a large Dublin pub where he was made manager in 1959. In 1960 he decided to give up pub work and seek a new life in London, where he got a job as a trainee in a stockbroker's office. He became deputy manager within five years and later became admin-head of international trading. In 1979, in partnership with 3 friends/colleagues, founded an international stockbroking company. They started that business from scratch, starting with 12 employees which grew to 500 within five years and with an annual turnover of between 10 and 15 billion pounds. That came to an end in 1991 when his partner and himself were arrested and charged with complex and serious fraud.

They were finally exonerated after 45 days in the dock at the central criminal court, but the business was destroyed. They won the case with costs. At the tender young age of 53 he found himself deprived of a future in financial services and unemployable so he needed to reinvent himself.

He lived in the south of France for a few years before moving to Uruguay for twenty years and eventually to Switzerland. During that time he formed a company with some mineral exploration technicians, geologists and engineers to explore for gold and copper deposits. They started in Chile where he spent 5 years driving the teams pickup truck, criss-crossing the Atacama Desert and driving on goat tracks at up to 10,000 feet in the Andes.

They expanded that to cover, Mexico, Canada, and West Africa. He gave up when the banks told him that they preferred to finance dot-com companies than mining companies.

He was now sixty and needed to reinvent himself again so he started an asset- management company which he ran until he was eighty.

Paddy has returned to Cahir almost every year to meet with his friends and when I asked him on looking back on his life if he had any advice for someone starting out...he said ..nothing is impossible..

THE TWO JOHNNIES

The duo Johnny B O'Brien from Cahir and Johnny McMahon from Roscrea are entertainers who had a meteoric rise to fame. The Cahir half comes from the famous hurley making families of the O'Briens of the Tipperary Road, his father Ger made hurleys and his grandfather before him carried on the trade on the road. The duo came from a humble band called Johnny B. and the Boogie Men, their popularity grew and grew and a stint on the national radio for two years did them no harm. This is yet another success story from some Cahir lads. They made it to Irish National television and there was no stopping them.

NEW SHOES

Pat Burke the blacksmith told me that one day a girl of about 16 years brought her pony to be shod, she said that daddy wanted shoes put on the pony's two back paws.

THE RYANS

Everybody would associate Paddy Ryan of Bengurrah with Cahir Park FC. Before moving to Bengurrah the Ryans lived in Market Street and worked in the mill like most of the town at the time the Cahir Mills were the big employers in the town. When the mills closed there was only one course to take and the emigrant ship was the way.

There were twelve in the family and Paddy's father chose New Zealand as the country to rear his children. A few years after getting work with a mining firm the father and five others were in a pickup travelling to work when an explosion caused the death of all five. His mother was left to carry on and raise the family. Paddy remained in Ireland to finish his apprenticeship as an electrician with Tom Samson. Tom himself emigrated to Canada shortly after.

Willie was in the Irish Army Band and bought himself out and went to New Zealand where he ended up in the country's National Orchestra.

All the Ryans played for the Cahir Park soccer team and John was no exception, after a while in New Zealand he played for the country's national team. He travelled the globe with them. Christie Ryan served his time at Baldonnel Airport and spent the rest of his working days at Wellington Airport in New Zealand.

MIDNIGHT MICKEY

Fred O Donnell lived in the Mall and had a Chemist Shop in Castle Street. He had among others his son Joe O' Donnell who was a prominent surgeon in Cork General Hospital. While Joe was going to college he worked his holidays with Colm Flynn the Vet. Michael O Donnell, his other son, remained living in the Mall for most of his adult life. Michael was a T.V. repairman and erected aerials on his own. His shop was on the Clonmel road. He could only erect the TV aerials at night because he was afraid of heights, he felt safe at night in the dark because he could not see the ground. This of course earned him the nickname of Midnight Mickey. He was one of nature's gentlemen.

GOING FAMILY

The Cahir mills as anyone of us can remember was the lifeblood of the town and lots of families slept under sheets with Balloon Flour half washed out of them.The flour bags were of pure cotton and families made them into bed sheets and pillows. Going and Smith were the owners at the time. The Goings of Cahir, owe their origins to Charles Going { 1763-1830 }.

He was the son of Giles Going and Sarah Reazon of Mountrath.

He made his fortunes in Cork as a merchant with a branch of the Quaker family of Fennells. In 1793 he married Hannah Clendennan of Mountrath. He later became a Quaker otherwise known as the Society of Friends. In 1798 Charles bought Suir Mill in Cahir and built Altavilla, a large residence on the Suir; this remained the principal seat of this branch of the Goings for nearly 150 years. Charles Going died in Cork in 1830 and his wife Hannah in Cahir in 1834.

Successive generations of Goings expanded their milling business after merging with the Smith family. In 1859 the Going and Smith firm came into being. The Cahir Abbey mills were for a long time owned by the Fennells and later Grubbs. The closure of these mills in the 1960s were a devastating blow to the town.

LOUGHLOHERY CASTLE

A 16 th. century tower that was owned by the Keating family, has four stories with the second story vaulted. There was also an attic in the roof which had gables on the four sides. The hall on the 3rd story had a fireplace as well as four gun loops. There is a drain for emptying chamber pots beside the loops. The fourth story contains two rooms.

There used to be a second identical castle directly across the road called Coolbane, that no longer exists. The field belongs to the famous John Anthony Hally. Ironically this field is called the Castle field even though the Castle is thrown down without a trace. Both Castles had a commanding view all over the countryside.

THE GOLDEN SEVEN

Around 1962 Oliver Colton arrived at his uncle's pub in Abbey Street.

He worked in the pub for a while and was a popular guy with all the customers. Oliver played the banjo and got it into his head to form a band, there were several musicians who frequented the bar and they practised in the covered space beside the pub. Those that I can remember were the Tommy [the Gag] Lonergan from Bengurrah a trombonist that was much in demand, all the big bands would have him if only he drank less. Jim Haide from Abbey Terrace, a postman on the drums, a man not averse to a pint. Oliver Colton on the banjo and Tom Hubbard a trumpet player who worked in the bakery. Bill Parfrey on piano and the inimitable Seanie Cunnigham on the melodeon. Breeda Carroll from Carrigeen supplied the vocals. Bridie Lonergan and Mary Brunnick were given the job of making sandwiches for the expected crowd and supplying bottles of stout to the band. They booked the parochial hall for the night. The excitement that this news generated is hard to believe. They estimated a crowd of 200 but in excess 1500 turned up and the hall could not hold the crowd. The merrymakers danced down the mall and the sandwiches were gone in a flash. The Gag for the first time in his life had access to free stout and he made the best of it. In the middle of a tune the Gag followed the trombone out over the stage and fell on the dancers below. The band had not a lot of energy left at 2 o'clock and the drummer fell over backwards and had to be carried home. The Golden Seven played only one night but they gave memories that were spoken about for years.

BURNCOURT CASTLE

This Castle was originally called Clogheen and the present name refers to its destruction by its owner Sir Richard Everard in 1650 to prevent it being occupied by Cromwellian troops. Sir Richard had only completed the house in 1641 and was hanged by General Ireton in 1651. The house was never restored despite being mostly sound.

MORE BENGURRITES

There was a scheme after the second World War to populate the likes of Australia, New Zealand and South Africa; it was called an assisted passage scheme. John Mahon, a brother of Paddy Mahon availed of the £10 fare and emigrated to Australia. John made for Melbourne in 1949 where he joined the Melbourne Police force. When he retired he was at the top of his profession, he retired a Chief Inspector and was stationed at Box Hill Police Station, Melbourne.

Another man from Bengurrah was Christie Hayes who was Station Master at Kings Cross Station in London, Chris never missed a year without coming home. Another school friend of ours was Michael Harris,,,nickname Yi Yi..who ran a well known pub for a lot of years in the centre of London..I think it was the ..Tom Cribb.

There was a priest that lived in Bengurrah ever before Fr. Joe Condon, called Fr. Dalton, who was a solitary figure that spent his time away in the Vatican, he returned annually and then nothing was ever heard of him again.

Every child that had a parents vocation as far as music was concerned went to Miss O Keefe, you daren't call her Monica. She was strict but as music teachers went she was the best. She put plastic sheets for the children to walk on and she used to sneak out back for a cigarette while the students were going through the scales. She always wore a long white shop coat that smelled of cigarettes. She never married and teaching music was all she did for a long long time.

ROOSCA AND ROCHESTOWN CASTLES

Roosca a 16th century castle belonging to the Burke clan, the structure is built on a rocky shelf high above the ground below and facing west.

It is also built above ground caves that are a danger to enter. The farmer's sheep are often lost underground. The Burke castle was captured in the 1640s and all the garrison and their families were put to death by Lord Inchiquin.

Rochestown castle in 1641, the Butlers besieged Thomas Grove here for five weeks until the walls were breached, a siege engine was used to breach the walls. In 1647 Lord Inchiquin again stormed and burned the castle and again killed the families and all the defenders.

THE COURTHOUSE ARDFINNAN

Along Ardfinnan's main street is the Boreen and a little way in is the Courthouse, now a private house and the occupier did not change the appearance of an almost old world structure. The last case that was heard was in 1919, and the last caretakers were the Maher family until 1890. The Petty Sessions were held every fortnight and the Magistrate used to bring his horse into the court with him. Those that were found guilty were brought out a narrow passage at the rear and led down beside the river to the waiting horse drawn Black Mariah and were transported into Clonmel Gaol. During the War of Independence the rebels used to hide arms and ammunition under the magistrates bench.

EDIE ROCHE

Edie Roche I suppose that her name was Edith, had a little shop on the Clonmel road. It was a great location when the Cinema was a few yards away. Edie always had a big smile and knew everyone in town.She was always singing and carried a mouth organ in her shop coat pocket. Edie'sbrother Billy had a shop on lower Abbey Street. In later years the shop was run by Breda Hennessey, a very good looking woman.

THE DEEP BLUE SEA

A most unusual occupation for a man from Cahir is a deep sea diver.

Jerry Sheehan Jnr. became a diver at the age of 28 and worked with maritime construction firms. He worked all over the world but mostly around the middle east, he tells me that the Persian Gulf is around 90 metres deep and that they were often down 300 metres in very cold water around Europe.

In extremely cold water they had hot water pumped around the diving suit, the air and water lines were attached to the oil platforms above.

He retired from diving at the age of 50 because of the dangers involved and he has had a few injuries. He said that every day you are always near an accident.

RUSSIAN - UKRAINE WAR

Russia declared war on Ukraine in February 2014 and they invaded Ukraine on 22 February 2022. With the result Europe was flooded with refugees and Ireland took their share of the misfortunate people. Allowing for the fact that we are part of the European Union the amount of different nationalities that made Ireland their home as, a recent poll tells us that there are 28 different nationalities attending the schools in Cahir. These are also different religions and there is never any problem.

The year is 2024 and the war is still raging

The Israel - Palestine conflict has been raging since October 2023 the barbarism continues in 2024.

John F O Gorman

John was reared close to New Inn, in Glennagat. His first wife was from Ardfinnan, named Margaret Smyth. Shortly after the first World War, John went to Germany and secured the first main dealership in Ireland for Mercedes - Benz cars. The O' Gormans had a Coachbuilding business in Prior Park in Clonmel. They manufactured horse traps and landaus and carriages as well as their main business building bus, coach, van and lorry bodies.

CASTLES OF CONSCIENCE

There are several houses in Clonmore that were built in the Victorian period, substantial solid cut stone buildings, that were made to last. The houses were referred to as Castles of conscience as they were a highly symbolic position for the residents. They were people that needed to be highly thought of. They, according to themselves, were above the ordinary working class, but could not quite make the company of the upper classes. This was during the reign of Victoria and we ask ourselves has anything changed in the new Millenium. To quote …Michael Foucault……A highly symbolic position, which will doubtless remain until our day, if we are willing to admit that what was a formerly visible fortress of order has now become a castle of conscience.

CAHIR FIRE BRIGADE

The old fire station used to be off Castle Street behind the old Garda Barracks. The fire station was moved to Barrack street to a purpose built structure. The fire men took delivery of a brand new Timoney fire engine in 1985. The fire station was in use until the new station was opened on the site of the old fire station on 23rd

April 1987. The site of the station is on Looby's field that was a playing field before the GAA acquired the present pitch. It was also used a few times a year for the Circus when it came to town. Up until recently the Firemen were unpaid volunteers but that evolved into a monetary reward for putting their lives on the line.

Back in the day there were a few characters with the brigade; one such member was drawing the blind pension; this was found out when he retired from the service as a volunteer. On another occasion no driver turned up to drive the fire engine, so a certain member attempted to drive the huge truck and it ended in disaster for a half dozen parked cars. The Firemen nowadays have to go through strict training for several weeks in Galway, they have to do water training for river rescuing and recovery, not a very pleasant prospect in winter. A fireman can no longer stay for as long as he likes, he has to retire now at 62.

THE PRINCE OF PIPERS

Edmund Keating Hyland was born in Cahir in 1780 and died in 1845. When he was 15 years old he contracted Smallpox and as a result it left him blind. His whole life was then devoted to the Uilleann Pipes and composing music. It is said that he was a world class player and a wonderful composer, he composed the famous jig the Fox Chase. among others. He performed before King George IV in 1821 and the King awarded him a set of new pipes worth 50 guineas.

Catherine Walsh known as Kitty the hare outside her house at
Sraid na Gcuic on the Tipperary road.

SENOR FOLI

Allan James Foley started life in Cahir in August 1837 before his parents emigrated to the USA, the Foley family lived in a lane at the rear of where the Credit Union building is now. Allan studied music in America and as his parents were fairly well off they sent Allan to Italy to continue his studies. He was by all accounts a great bass opera singer. He kept the sound of his name but changed the spelling to Foli, as was the Italian way, he became known all over the globe.

He had a varied career and had a gift for making money. He was an inveterate gambler but successful at it and he was very successful on the stock exchange. When he died he left his wife very well off.

He was one of the first musicians to make a phonograph recording with other famous female opera singers at Crystal Palace in London and subsequently taking the recordings back to America with him, alas no account of them can now be found. Senor Foli died suddenly at Southport in Oct. 1899.

The great Count John Mc Cormack, another famous singer, met and married Lilly Foley the sister of the aforementioned Senor Foli.

Desiree Clary whose father was Cleary from
Carrigatha OF GARNIVILLA

Who was Kate of Garnivilla.? She was Kate Nagle who lived from 1793 to 1862 and was well known for her beauty in her younger days.

The story goes that Edward Lysaght was visiting Garnavilla when he saw young Kate at an upstairs window as he was approaching on his horse and the sight of her beauty had a lasting effect on him.

Edward became a barrister and as far as we can tell Kate of Garnivilla was the only poem that he wrote in Irish. It has been translated into English on many occasions as well as been set to music. Garnivilla is still standing and is still occupied. The Nagle family tomb is in Rochestown a short distance from Garnivilla. In the Inch Field at the rear of Cahir Castle is a tree trunk carved by Philip Quinn with a few lines from the poem.

The house was subsequently owned by the Nolan family famed in British military circles. Spear Nolan was a first world war veteran and was descended from a long line of people in military life.

BURKE'S FORGE.

Maurice…Mossie…Casey

Maurice spent his youth in Ballyboy, Clogheen. His primary school days were spent in Duhill National school. The affection that he holds for that area is still very strong. Such memories still exist today. The community spirit has remained active with a fabulous community centre to compensate for the loss of venues like pubs in rural areas.

Mossie's father worked as a groom for Grubbs of Castlegrace and trained horses for different owners. Mossie was always involved with him in the training of the horses. To this day he loves being around horses. The horse that he rides out on to this day, came first in the qualifiers for the RDS performance class and went on to take second place competing in the RDS.

The first racehorse that Mossie purchased was ..Casey Tiles.. who represented his business and acted as a source of advertising, went on to win races in Ireland and Wales and was trained by Danny O Connell.

The horse ..Casey Tiles..happened to be a granddaughter of the famous Saddlers Wells. As it happens, Saddlers Wells is the only horse that Coolmore Stud preserved in their museum.

The second racehorse that he purchased was from David Murnane and was trained by David, was called ..Settle for Red.. This horse again went on to win many races.

Mossie's Third racehorse..Settle for Bay.. was jointly owned by Mossie and Denis McGettigan, again purchased from David Murnane who trained him and went on to win four races in a row in Ireland that qualified him to run in the Royal Ascot Hunt Cup at Ascot. Settle for Bay was entered in a field of 30 runners, beating them all and winning a very prestigious race for his owners. This win gave Mossie such excitement and pleasure. The 16-1 winner cleaned out the bookies in Cahir, Cashel,

Mitchelstown and Tipperary town.

The Casey family lived in Ballyboy until Mossie was 14 and the family then moved to Ballydavid, Bansha. His mother had the family kneeling down every night saying the Rosary in the hope of owning their own home. Many a night the mother fell asleep saying the Rosary.

Owning their own home in Ballydavid made her dream come true.

Whenever Mossie's mother fell asleep, the children had great fun asking the neighbours to pray for them instead of the saints. He recalls one of the neighbours felt that he had a direct line to Heaven and to neighbours that had passed away. This neighbour used to inform them of how the Gaa teams were performing in Heaven.

The home that the Casey family had in Ballydavid was previously an RIC Barracks and to this day has a prison cell and gate. The house is now being renovated by Mossie's nephew Ronan Casey and girlfriend, the family are delighted to see it coming back to life.

Mossie's Father worked for Major Pidcock at Scarrough Wood on the outskirts of Cahir. The Major purchased a horse called ..Captain Christy who went on to win the Cheltenham Gold Cup.

Mossie still has a silver box and a note presented by the Major to his father in appreciation for looking after the great Captain Christy.

Mossie attended Cahir Tech and at eighteen years old, headed to London where he worked in a watch and dial factory and went on to manage the factory after one year. A few years later Mossie started his own flooring business in London and at twenty eight years sold up the business to return to Cahir. He started a contract business supplying and fitting carpets, tiles and floor coverings operating from a hay barn behind Church Street, Cahir. After Mossie purchased 28 acres from Paddy Devereux on the Tipperary Road which became the first Business Park of its type in Co Tipperary. Cahir Business Park continues to be developed today and has in excess of 300 people working there. Casey Tiles and wood floors were the first warehouses to be built in the park and companies like T.J O'Mahony's, Murphy Candles,

Horizon Steel Framed Manufacturers, Buttimer Engineering, Dalton Transport, Dan Casey and many others.

Mossie stayed single until he was thirty eight as he enjoyed the single life of fast horses, fast cars and fast dancers. Brendan Behan said he was a drinker with a writing problem, Mossie recons that he is a dancer with a work problem.

Approximately 20 years after the fire in the Mill building on Church Street there was a proposal to demolish it. Mossie purchased it and had it restored, retaining all its original character. He also bought another derelict building and yard on Abbey Street and brought it back to life by building 15 apartments and a commercial building currently occupied by Boyle Sports and Sharon Rossiter Accountancy. Mossie had the pleasure of being involved in many Charitable organisations such as the Day Care Centre, The Youth Centre and was on the board of Aiseiri Rehabilitation Centre. In one fundraiser for the Day Care Centre, Mossie cycled through Cambodia and Vietnam, not an easy task in those temperatures.

Mossie went on to have two children, Anne Marie and Maurice Jnr.

Or as Mossie used to call him when he was little..Morris Minor…

He is very proud of his children as both went down the academic route and did not join their father in his business ventures. Their father supported their decision to paddle their own canoes.

Maurice Jnr. did do a half days work as a young teenager in Casey Tiles.

He was blowing up footballs for a promotion, inside the cardboard boxes Maurice found a label stating that there was no child labour in the production of these footballs. He brought this to his fathers attention and promptly resigned from his bright future in Casey Tiles.

THE CASEY CHILDREN

Anne Marie, daughter of Mossie and Josephine went on to become a school teacher and later married and has a family.

Maurice Jnr. went from refusing to blow up footballs to doing his BA at Trinity College Dublin and then onto Jesus College Oxford where he was a PHD candidate. And if that wasn't enough he received an Mphil from the university of Cambridge. He attended Stanford, the Centre for Russian, East European and Eurasian studies. He then did Postdoctoral Researcher, Historian at Queen's University Belfast. At the time of writing he has a book launch of,,, Hotel Lux in Dublin and Cahir.

AHOY ARDFINNAN

Another unusual occupation for an inland county like Tipperary is a man whose mother is from Ardfinnan. Mary Kavanagh's [Norris] son Liam qualified and passed his marine exams, Liam became the youngest Ship's Captain in Ireland. He was on board oil tankers for some time and he sailed the Jeanie Johnson, the famous Famine Ship to America.

Not satisfied with sailing the seven seas Liam turned his attention to the air and went about doing the exams for his commercial pilots licence.

Cahir Park House ablaze 1963

ROBBIE O DWYER

Another Cahir man is 36 year old Robbie O'Dwyer, son of Alan and Noleen, who has an unusual way of making a living. He is a voiceover artist that does the voices for cartoons and advertising promotions. Robbie began this unusual hobby while he was in Cahir and to broaden his chances of getting work he moved to Canada. He keeps sending his work to all the big studios in hope of getting the big break. We can only wish him the best and hope he makes the big time.

James Cody and Jude the Two. Cahir 1900.

JOHN ANTHONY HALLY

At the time of writing in 2024 our man John is 87 years and comes from Loughloher, one could call him a farmer that collects and hoards machinery. At his big age he insists on doing everything on his own. The machinery is as old as himself, he drives an old David Brown 990 and has a Marshall tractor in perfect condition. We called to see him but he was gone saving hay at 6 o'clock in the evening planning to work all night. His neighbour said of John …he is the only man that gave two days fixing the lights on the tractor to work one night. John is a great source of information about times gone by.

Opening night advert in Nationalist 1961.

JUDE THE TWO AND JAMES CODY

The story behind the famous photo, is for a start the two that are pictured together, are actually at each side of the road. They were vicious deadly enemies and hated each other. The photo was taken by P.J Condon of Church Street, he asked Jude to pose for him and by accident James Cody walked into the picture. P.J would not waste an opportunity like this and got the only chance at the entrance to Pearce Street.

It is lost to posterity as to the reason for their bad feelings towards each other. Jude walked the town selling her wares from a basket, Clothes pegs matches and handkerchiefs and so on. James Cody played a hurdy gurdy, a hand wound music box.The photo has been used many times over the years, in other countries since 1900.

Jerry Sheehan outside his shop in the Square late 1930s.

PILLARS

STANDING STONES AT
SIR R. PEEL
M.P.
Died July 2, 1850
Aged 62 years
JOHN CUSACK
PROPRIETOR
D. O. CONNELL
Esq. M.P.
Died in Genoa
May 13th 1847
JOHN CUSACK
PROPRIETOR
MONARAHA
BALLYMACADAM

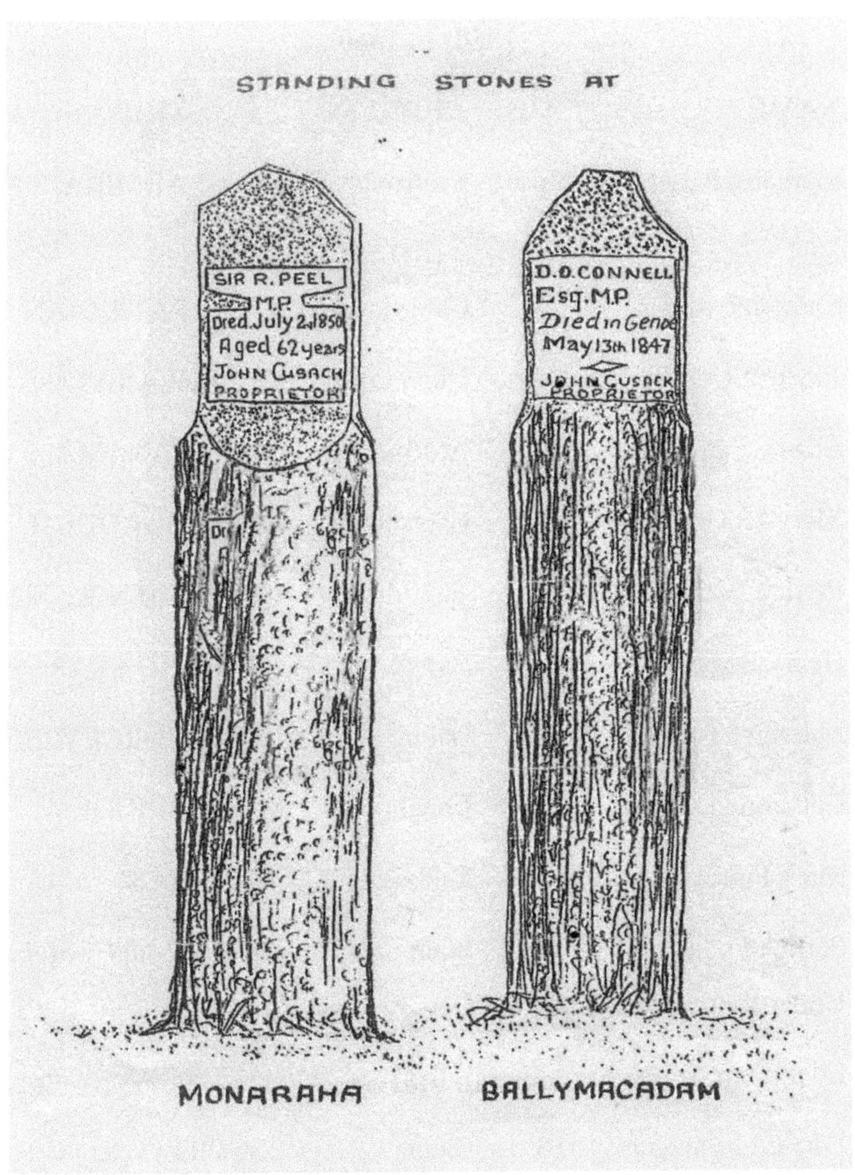

EMIGRANTS FROM CAHIR TO AUSTRALIA

1850s to 1860s

NAME	AGE	ADDRESS	SHIP
Margaret Roache LYONS	16	Scarrough Wood	ADMIRAL
Catherine Regan	18	Cahir town	PATRICIAN
Johanna Costello	19	Clonmore.	WANATA
Eliza Landregan	47	Ardfinnan.	PANAMA
Mary McGrath	23	Cahir town	ELLENBOROUGH
Patrick Wall	23	Tubrid.	QUEEN OF ENGLAND
Henry Bevans	17	Ballyboy.	MORNING STAR
Margaret Torpy	11	Cahir.	MONTMORCEY
Catherine Dower	17	Loughryan.	WOODBRIDGE
Mary Farrel	26	Kilmoyler.	ATHENIAN
Patrick Fogarty	19	Stammers very much could not be Understood. From Cahir.	
Ellen Lane	13	Cahir.	PALMYRA
Edward Lonergan	16	Cahir	ESCORT.

9 781917 505710